Marilyn,
The view is great from
the top - Blessings!
Stan Farmer

FOOL

ON

A

HILL

by

Stan Farmer

Front and back covers are original artwork by:
Jon Allan Marshall.
Mr. Marshall may be contacted at:
RR#1 Box 977
Denmark, ME 04022
email: <marshall@pivot.net>

Published in the
United States of America by:
Bellbuoy Books, a division of;
Tidal-Tale Books, LLC
Wolf Hill Road-PO Box 624
Hillsboro, NH 03244
stan@bellbuoy.com

Printed in the United States

FOOL ON A HILL is a human interest story; a strong, encouraging, honest story. It is intended to inspire, enlighten, and instruct.

FOOL ON A HILL contains lessons for each stage of life—from snotty-nose kid to reflective Senior. It is a story about:

- conclusions and conundrums
- courage and fear
- questions and answers—sometimes no answers!
- heroic achievements and dismal failures
- life-ruining choices and miraculous recoveries

FOOL ON A HILL is about rejection, rebellion, and redemption. About mercy and grace. Hope.

PREFACE

FOREWARD

"Raising young men and women to lives of adult responsibility has never been easy. This book won't necessarily make it easier but it will be of great encouragement. In matters of God's sovereignty you'll learn a fundamental truth: God is ultimately victorious although He doesn't always make everything less difficult along the way. If the road you travel has been bumpy, learn from a believable fellow traveler who has been through potholes and over bumps that make your's look like cracks and pebbles, and throughout he never lost his sense of humor. The reader also lives through the exciting development of "His Mansion"--a place of healing and rehabilitating love for needy young adults."

Dr. C. Everett Koop,
former United States
Surgeon General

FOREWARNING!

The thesis of *Fool on a Hill* is to encourage, to inspire, and to teach lessons of value. Friends have encouraged and prodded me to write this book for years. Most wanted it to be a "how to" manual. Co-founding a work dedicated to help hurting and traumatized young adults and traveling as extensively as I have for thirty years, surely I must have discovered the key to successful living. Wrong!

I am neither a gifted counselor nor psychologist. Certainly, I have made most of the same mistakes and committed many of the same sins as my fellow man. My father was fond of the comment, "The best way to learn is from experience and fools learn by no other." Truth be known; I've learned most of my lessons the hard way. A fool, indeed!

I'm not a great "how-to" guy. I'm still learning. However, there is a story to be told. My intent is that you might be encouraged, inspired--even learn something valuable--by observing some of my friends and me as we make our way from sea-level to mountain heights. You needn't get *too* close or "do what I do,"--that could be disastrous--'tis better to just observe. I have made choices you would not--should not--make, but by observing you can prepare yourself to make healthier choices when you arrive at the inevitable fork in the road.

Perhaps a history or a biographical treatise? No, I don't wish to look back too much, except to learn. Hope and excitement always lie ahead. It has not been my intention to allow too much of me to clutter this thing, except to the extent that I've been a part of it. The markers and milestones along the way represent what I suspect have characteristics typical of most of our lives. Enjoy!

ACKNOWLEDGMENTS

All of the personal stories are taken from the lives of real people, most of whom have allowed me to use their actual names. In some cases, I've chosen not to use their actual name because I felt that it would not prudent. In regards to this book, the biggest debt of gratitude is owed to those allowing their stories to be told. There are folks whom I've encountered along my journey who weren't asked how they would prefer me to treat them. They are extremely important to this book. My wife Joan, my children, and a number of others have paid dearly for reckless forays down dead-end paths. The debt to them cannot be adequately repaid. I thank them for their grace and where it is appropriate, ask for their forgiveness.

I made a new friend in the process of writing, which was an unexpected bonus. I needed help--lots of help. Research and interviews of people featured in the book required gobs of time and travel. My duties as CEO and President of His Mansion did not permit me to cover all of the bases. A young woman who was finishing her commitment at His Mansion and returning to the marketplace, came to my rescue. An aspiring writer!

Caryn Pederson is a graduate of Wheaton College ('95) with a Masters in Intercultural Communications. The initial product of one of her interviews set me upright! *This lady can write!* Her first rough drafts were better than my finished product.

Caryn was eager to help me, but she had lots of reservations! We could not be more unalike in temperament and taste. She is a stickler for detail and accuracy. Her expectations were very high--for her work--and of me as a co-worker. Nearly every time we interacted during the first month, I provoked her to tears. At one point, I even shed a few!

I am a better writer today because of Caryn's contribution. There was much more to learn from her than I had to teach her. Caryn's fingerprints are all over this book. I could not have continued the effort without her help. That she could've written such a book alone, I have no doubt. I could not have. I predict that one day "Caryn Pederson" will be a familiar name to many readers.

Caryn is presently the Assistant for Communications with PIONEERS, a missions organization dedicated to planting churches among unreached peoples and has several writing assignments in the works.

Fool on a Hill is a personal, private effort. I am indebted to the Board of Directors of His Mansion Ministries for the grace and flexibility granted me. I didn't have a clue how much work writing a book would be. For three years--weekends, vacations, travel time, and comptime--I have been engaged in making it into a reality.

His Mansion Ministries has not commissioned this work, nor underwritten the costs of producing it. Responsibility for anything written in this book lay solely with the author. His Mansion Ministries, nor its Officers, have endorsed or subsidized its publication.

DEDICATION

I dedicate this book to my wife of forty years. Joan has paid a much higher price for my story than anyone should. His Mansion as it is, would not be, except for her perseverance and dependence upon God. The role she has played in my life, His Mansion's history, and in the lives of many who've served here is deeper and wider than could be seen by most of the people who have encountered us along the journey. She is loved by her children, grandchildren--and by me! Thank you, Joan.

PROLOGUE

VIEW FROM THE HILL

The scene takes place as the rauckous and radical sixties run out of breath and staggers into the depressed seventies. Two doors away from where I sit enjoying ham 'n eggs, homefries and coffee, stands a huge, gray building with a weathered sign declaring the building to be the Valley Inn, Hillsborough, Hew Hampshire. It boasts of twenty-five rooms, a restaurant, and sitting rooms, but for the last year it stood eerily silent. Once-upon-a-time, it had been the traveler's choice and the center of social commerce. Before stopping for breakfast my curiosity got the best of me and I peeked through the dirt-encrusted glass to see a turn-of-the-century reservation desk, ornate molded tin ceilings, and a magnificent fireplace. Fuel is expensive, jobs scarce, and business ventures are risky. The old girl awaits the mercy of a wrecking ball to finish her off while she still has a certain dignity.

It's a shame because this town needs to hold on to every scrap of dignity that remains. The sheep, that populated the surrounding hillsides fifty years ago, now live in New Zealand and the mills that once turned the wool into yarn can now be found in Georgia. The landmark coveredbridge that carried passenger trains and freight cars over the river twice a day has become the favorite haunt of partying teenagers. The river that once provided energy and life to factories and families at the turn of the century now passes through town as quickly as it comes, much like the tourists and travelers who pass through on their way to more attractive destinations.

The view from my breakfast booth at the Copper Lantern reveals a main street lined with buildings marred by broken and bordered windows, the sobering evidence of ill-conceived, under-financed business ventures. A once grand show-theater stands like an elegant lady whose time and good fortune have long since passed. One side of the derelict hulk offers as "antiques," artifacts that in twenty years will still barely qualify for roadside flea markets. The other side of the building attempts to make it as a bar, yet even the promise of escape within its dark interior fails to arouse much interest in this depressed, dying village.

Except for the tall spire on the traditional, white community congregational church, this forgotten mill town bears little resemblance to the quaint, picture-postcard villages imagined by those who live outside of New England. But my eyes are drawn to the east, across a bridge, where the landscape rises gradually to twin peaks that seem to beckon: "Come, rise above, escape." I begin my journey up.

As the country road reaches its zenith and gives way to the first, slight downgrade, a tree-lined dirt road breaks abruptly to the right inviting me to enter. I am drawn. Barely out of sight of the paved road, I discover myself in a secluded, New England village, one that does do the postcards justice: A sanctuary.

I pass a white clapboard house with four great pillars and black numerals boasting a 1767 birthdate. Opposite this historic building sits a picture-perfect barn of the same vintage. A chapel, several quaint village houses, cabins, and dormitories—all white—are scattered about the hillside. A large dining hall, a sugar-shed, and more than a hundred cord of firewood line the path, giving me the sensation of having stepped back 100 years in time.

Though there are no sounds or signs of life on this day, my imagination is stirred by forces outside of intellect. The landscape is transformed. I can envision strawberry patches being picked over by young women who sing and laugh together. Black and white cows amble to the fence, necks arched upward expecting to be scratched--totally without fear of my presence. The air is alive with the sounds of life. An old John

Deere 320 patiently makes its way across a field. Pop...pop...pop! A 30-inch steel disk sporting formidable teeth whines its way through solid oak.

I can almost hear children laughing and playing near a small pond where bullfrogs urge them on. Young women tend flower gardens and men move about carrying lumber or leading calves. A brace of red Devon oxen lumber along in graceful unison, pulling a scoot-load of cordwood to an awaiting shed.

The rutted, rock-strewn road surrenders its identify to a well-worn path that urges me further up the mountainside where there are no more buildings. The imagined sounds of humanity fade to silence as I trek farther up the hill.

From the pinnacle of this granite-crowned summit I can see 360 degrees. To the northeast, the summits of Mt. Washington and the Presidential Range are clear. To the north, Mt. Kearsarge and Mt. Sunapee mark the southern edge of the White Mountain Range. To the southwest, Mt. Monadnock, the most climbed mountain in the country, stands proud.

My reverie is jarred by the realization that I am, in fact, not standing on granite at all, but on bronze! There is a three-by-five-foot plaque directly beneath my feet. It reads:

******

CLARK SUMMIT
by act of the New Hampshire Legislature
January Session 1951
Here Clark Poling loved to be;
Here he found himself.
Clark Vandersoll Poling
Columbus, Ohio   August 7, 1910
North Atlantic   February 3, 1943

"Clark Poling was a boy of this town.
As he grew older he was a friend
and leader of Deering boys."

CITATION FOR THE DISTINGUISHED SERVICE CROSS

Chaplain (first lieutenant) Clark Vandersoll Poling, Army of the United States. For extraordinary heroism in connection with military operations against the enemy of the United States, on the night of 3 February 1943. A loaded troop transport was torpedoed without warning by an enemy submarine in the North Atlantic and began to sink rapidly. In the resulting confusion and darkness some men found themselves without life jackets and others became helpless through fear and the dread of plunging into the freezing water. Chaplain Poling heroically and calmly moved about the deck encouraging men and assisting them to abandon ship. After the available supply of life jackets was exhausted, he gave up his own. He remained aboard ship and went down with it offering words of encouragement and prayers to the last.

******

Clark Poling, a bright young man of privilege, pedigree, and superior education, once stood where I am standing. The promise of family and personal achievement lay before him. But for all the disciplines and opportunities available to him, he chose to represent the love and grace of God to men who lived in constant fear of death and loss. When a lifejacket meant the difference between life and death, there was no hesitation. He died that another might live. Clark's contagious laugh—heard even in his final moments—rings in the memory of a Dorchester survivor. *

Poling, as a youngster had spent many hours meditating on this very spot. Surely, a fool had stood on this hill! I stand here now...

Nearly three decades later, from the same vantage point on the summit, the once forlorn town in the valley below appears transformed. The lively community nestled on a plateau three-quarters of the way up a mountain, once merely a product of my vivid imagination, has become a reality known as His Mansion.

Imagining all this from my hilltop perch might seem the momentary idle fantasy of a foolish dreamer, but my pilgrimage to this special place began long before my morning cup of coffee. As a young man of thirty I made the decision to leave the clearly mapped and predictable path through life for a more exciting adventure

* Poling, Daniel, *Mine Eyes Have Seen the Glory*, McGraw-Hill: New York, 1959, 204.

I. HOME GROWN

The years spent in and around the nest are filled with a thousand experiences—good and bad. We all start at a point not of our own choosing. Specific events and our encounters with influential people naturally incline us toward predictable destinations. Certainly the encounters and experiences make up the raw material, but they needn't predetermine whom we become.

"Hey Bub, get up. Get up. Wake up. Give your Dad a big hug and a kiss. I'll write, and before you know it, I'll be back."

On a dismal, foggy morning I watched out the window as the man I loved most in this world—the only man I really knew at that time—headed down the hill with a large, white canvas seabag over his shoulder. The bounce in his step told me it wasn't as difficult for him to leave as it was for me to watch him go.

I knew at least two weeks prior, that this day was coming. My Dad's temperament had improved, his drinking lessened, and there was a sense of adventure in the air. That was always his way just before he shipped out on a tanker or freighter and for several days a large oil tanker lay at anchor between Peaks Island and Portland.

This morning as I fought crawling out from under the warm blankets I heard a series of throaty blasts of a ship's whistle signaling the two or three crewmen who lived on the island that it was time to embark. Down in the harbor the Harris Oil Company work boat swung idly on her mooring, waiting to ferry the crewmen to the ship.

Later, as I kicked a stone along the road to school, I listened for the single long, mournful blast of the ship's whistle which exclaimed to all that she was weighing anchor and getting underway. Each time a tanker slipped out of the harbor with my dad aboard, part of me slipped away too.

It was the mid-40's, the war years, and the presence of this powerfully influential person I called dad was sporadic and unpredictable. Although Dad might be amused to discover who else *joins* him in my album of influential people, he remains the star.

* * *

Long before I embarked upon a journey toward the hill, I learned a number of powerful, life-shaping lessons like the

2

one that took place in a unique setting on Peaks Island, Maine where I grew up. A favorite childhood haunt was out on the end of the ledge at Whitehead Passage near the convent. Sitting on the outermost point of the narrow finger of granite, I was less than a quarter mile away from a small, but high, grassy islet known as "Pumpkin Knob." Early in June of each year an immature whale appeared. I marked the day she arrived, and the following year counted the days until she returned. Always, within a day or two of the previous year's arrival, she surfaced again. I was awed by her size and power, but especially impressed by her clever feeding routine.

When the squid and mackerel were running, the porpoises would charge the currents and ride over the submerged ledges like marauding knights, racing to see which one could corral and devour the most bait fish. As the current drove fish through the narrows between the island and Pumpkin Knob, the growing whale would position herself facing the current at the outflow of the gut, straining the fish from the water. As soon as the tide reversed itself and began flowing in earnest in the opposite direction, she would appear on the other end for the second course of her meal! The whale seemed uniquely equipped to thrive in her vast, yet highly defined environment. The world I was growing up in was far more complex, however. My whale friend simply took in what she was fed. I also took in everything that came my way. How I responded to the experiences forced upon me would, in the final analysis, prepare me for my unique journey through life. Lessons-by-the-seas were profound and nearly always safe, but the most vivid, and sometimes most painful, always involved people!

Another entry in my album of influential people was Weird Willy, but gaining an audience with him could be dangerous. The warning call, "It's the Foleys!" could send young boys scurrying faster than cottontail rabbits catching the scent of the wily, old red fox. There were twelve or thirteen Foleys, all redheaded and freckle-faced, ferocious and mean. You could be assured of a pummeling if any two of them came upon you. That was a problem because the Foleys were always referred to in the plural—there was no such thing as one Foley!

The shortcut from school cut across the ridge of the island right in front of the Foleys' large, dilapidated house. Several of us would risk the hazard of going past the Foley den each week in the hopes that we might spend time with Weird Willy. No, Willy was not the family mastiff, but a shell-shocked World War II veteran who I'd always assumed "belonged" to the Foleys. Willy held court on the porch of the Foley house in an old wicker-bottomed rocker. He was the island's own rocking-chair philosopher.

Incredibly gullible and naive, Willy believed every crazy story we told him. He patiently listened to our cruel litany of lies and fantasies only to attempt to top our stories with his tales of sea monsters, ghosts in the night, and secret communities which he alone visited, far beneath the granite dome of our island. To boys whose dads were dead war heroes or absent at sea for months, Willy was loved and appreciated despite the fact that he was mentally impaired—or perhaps because of it. Oh, the miracle of being listened to and taken seriously! While dads were at sea, Grandfathers, aged Uncles, and the occasional Weird Willy, became the male role models who provided an essential link to the world of grown men.

Even in the social isolation of an island, one of the most colorful influences in life came from across a cultural divide. In my case, that influence came from the other side of a barbed-wire fence. The fence kept the U. S. Army on one side, and civilians on the other. The military personnel were there to guard the huge 16-inch cannons poised in constant vigil over the entrance channel to Portland Harbor during W.W. II. In the late '40s, Sergeant Gancy arrived to replace the man who had been in charge since the end of the war. The new overseer

4

brought with him a wife and a ten-year-old daughter, Stephanie. The Gancys quickly became the talk of the island. Sergeant Gancy was a highly decorated veteran of W.W. II. He was also a black man—the first I'd ever seen. He had met and married a fraulein while stationed in Germany. I first saw Stephanie when she showed up for school several days after their arrival.

I was immediately taken with Stephanie. Of course on an island where few could remember ever seeing a person of color, this should come as no surprise. Aside from her chocolate colored skin, her nose and smile were the next features to catch my attention. Her smile was captivating. This girl beamed. No one I'd ever met displayed so many teeth with a simple smile.

Stephanie was born in Germany, which greatly added to her mystique. She had also lived in California and I had never met anybody who had been out of Maine—except my dad. This girl had been everywhere and knew about things of which I had only dreamed or heard stories about. She fascinated me.

It became evident in subsequent weeks that my attraction to Stephanie Gancy was not sitting well with my friends or their parents. I began to hear children calling her "Hershey Bar." At first it wasn't clear to me why this nickname moved her to tears. Every island youngster earned a nickname sooner or later, but I didn't like to see her crying. I was bothered because I couldn't understand why she should be so upset. To my way of thinking, Hershey Bars were pretty hot items! I had only had one or two in my entire life; candy was a luxury. The negative connotation of having the color of one's skin compared to chocolate was lost on me.

It soon became apparent that these comments and nicknames were *intended* to be derisive—to hurt. I knew my schoolmates well enough to know they weren't bright enough to come up with these painful barbs by themselves. They must have been hearing this talk at home.

5

Before their first Christmas, the Gancys requested an early transfer and left the island, taking my new friend with them, but I was left with a positive impression of what Stephanie-sort-of-people were like. They were happy, smiling, world-traveled, and expansive. I was prepared to like them and I was not disappointed by my next encounter with a person of color.

On special occasions, Dad would invite me to accompany him on trips to the mainland to do errands in the city. He always began the day's outing by making the early crossing. The adventure would include having breakfast at the Port Hole Diner, a hole-in-the-wall eatery located behind Custom House wharf. That's where the stevedores, boat crews, canning plant workers, and longshoremen gathered.

Everyone knew and respected my dad. He had fought Golden Gloves in the Navy and was a veteran of occasional battles outside the ring as well. These same men had witnessed some of these unofficial bouts. Theirs was a respect born out of fear and admiration, perhaps spiced with a dash of disapproval, but respect all the same. I sensed their admiration as I stood proudly beside my dad as we exited the crowded restaurant and continued our trip "uptown."

While walking with Dad along Congress Street that morning, I had my second encounter with a black person. He was ebony black and wore a tight-fitting tank top. Immediately my mind raced to a National Geographic with drawings depicting Africans being taken into slavery. It was all I could do to tear my eyes from him. Dad pulled me around and we continued our walk, but the questions followed. This man evoked a different image than did my island friend and her father.

Dad had lived and worked all over the world with men of every color and culture, and he willingly answered my flood

6

of questions. Nothing in his explanations left me with a hint of the prejudice my schoolmates had gleaned from their parents regarding the Gancys, nor did it incline me toward the sort of prejudice I would witness in future years.

The huge black man was "Smitty" Hicks. Smitty, as it turned out, was a respected acquaintance of my dad's and a close friend of my aunt and uncle. Smitty and his wife, Dottie, owned the apartment house on Boyd Street where my Aunt Gladys and Uncle John Calvert were tenants. When I visited Aunt Gladys, I occasionally had a ringside seat at one of Smitty and Dot's fights. My Italian friends' families yelled and argued a lot—what they called fighting—but the Hicks' knew how to fight! Back in my Irish clan, we called this sort of family squabble a "donnybrook."

On one such occasion, Smitty came home drunk having been out drinking for days. Dot was so angry that she went after him without a hint of fear. She drove Smitty right out the door onto the sidewalk wielding a paring knife she'd been using to peel potatoes. This especially impressed me because Smitty was the current heavyweight boxing champion of Maine! My dad and I occasionally went to see him fight on Saturday nights at the Expo. Later that night, Smitty and Dot made up as if nothing had ever happened.

In another memorable incident, the sight of a huge needle wielded by a foreign-looking man had the same effect upon me as Dot's paring knife had on Smitty. A dental training school was located on India Street in Portland. Poor families brought their children there for free treatment providing the trainees with "guinea pigs" on which to practice.

Attempting to imitate the comic book Tarzan swinging on a vine, I'd collided with a tree--teeth first. One tooth had turned black, so mom and I took the early ferry to the mainland, and walked from there to the "clinic." As if the cold, white enamel dental chair were not intimidating enough, a dark man speaking perfect English in a singsong cadence fastened his black eyes upon me. With one hand behind his back, he proceeded straight toward me. As his hand came from its hiding place, I spotted the needle. It looked more like an ice pick! I panicked and leaped from the chair with no intention of getting back into it.

Mom jerked me by one ear lobe and then the other all the way from India Street, across town, then to Back Bay where my aunt Gladys lived. By the time we arrived, both my earlobes were ripped to the cup.

Aunt Gladys was quick to take upon herself my shame, hurt, and pain. She was born "tongue-tied" and as a child had been labeled "retarded"--which of course, she was not. Today, her condition is recognized as a cleft palate and is known to have little influence upon one's intelligence. But a lifetime of rejection and being ridiculed left her acutely sensitive to the underdog, which in this case was me. Oh, the thrill and the wonder of being fought for and defended with loving compassion. If only the world were amply supplied with such special people. Aunt Gladys taught me much. Her act of love cemented our relationship and continues to inspire me. Fortunately, there would be others to follow who were strategically placed along the road to encourage me.

"FARMER! Come to my office right now!" The terrifying bass voice of the principal so alarmed the members of study hall that the girl opposite me lost control of her bladder. A canyon-deep voice was the trademark of the silver-haired retired naval commander, Charles Delano. His portrait stands out in my album of influential people. My own reaction to his ultimatum was tempered by the fact that "Charley" had been my agriculture teacher for several years prior to his becoming a principal. Aggie teachers, like industrial arts teachers, band directors, and coaches, develop a much different relationship with their students. He was in a better position to influence me than any of my academic instructors.

I knew Mr. Delano as someone more than a harsh task-master, so it was his demeanor more than his voice that convinced me something serious was up. The hallway was empty by the time I rushed through the double doors, but no problem, I knew my way to "the office" by heart! Mr. D. dismissed his secretary and the gaggle of girls who seem to fill pet positions in every high school office in America. We were alone. With doors closed, he began in his patented deep, slow, controlled voice, "Mr. Farmer, I hear you are about to be dismissed from this school for academic failure."

"Yes, sir," I replied.

"Look here, Farmer, do you see this shoe? (A size fourteen, I estimated.) The next time you see it, it will be substantially buried in your hind end! I will not allow you to quit or to be thrown out. You have the stuff to be someone special and to do something of significance. Get out of my office and I'll see you at graduation."

This encounter proved to be a pivotal point in my life—not because I feared the man's boot, but because someone I trusted, respected, and believed in, believed in me and said I had "the stuff." I had no idea what "the stuff" was and am still not sure today, but it must be good!

I managed to break away from the peer group to which I had attached myself, perhaps even helped create. I studied hard and pulled my grades up to barely passing. I graduated with my class and was awarded the "Anchor Award" for the lowest possible passing grade by none other than Mr. Charles Delano, Commander, USN, ret. The lessons learned in the principal's office were positive and became points of reference later in life.

*   *   *

As a youngster I'd learned to survive abrupt and disconcerting changes, but unlike my whale model who readily

9

adapted to changing tides according to some prehistoric program, adapting to some of the changes I experienced in life was disturbing and the appropriate response didn't always come naturally.

Alcohol could turn my #1 hero into Mr. Hyde. Dad and old man Tuttle, from downstreet, had been hard into the homemade dandelion wine. Dr. Jekyll left our house that afternoon. Mr. Hyde returned.

Ripping the phone from the wall, dad crowded us into an anteroom at gunpoint while he ranted on about life's injustices. The actual words accompanying this frightening event have long since evaporated, but I remember the sense of fear as if it were yesterday. Alcohol had turned a powerful, intelligent man into a blubbering, self-pitying, dangerously suicidal stranger.

I had seen the drunken version before, but he usually left us in tension between laughter and disgust. I remember the day I was sent out in search of Dad and my adopted Irish uncle, "Dud-o." After an afternoon of "Black and Tans," Dad had set out to take Dud-o home in an old steel wheelbarrow. On the way, both of them had passed out in an orchard amid decaying apples. I wasn't strong enough to handle one of them in the wheelbarrow, to say nothing of two. So I rescued the wheelbarrow!

When husbands and fathers go off to sea for prolonged periods, many of them resort to alcohol the entire time they are ashore. Young men in these communities tend to grow up fast, and that makes life particularly difficult for girls entering their teens.

Life on our island was no exception. No matter how hard the girls tried to maintain their reputation, some brainless, senseless, young turk would spread a story that was soon accepted as truth. Unfortunately, some girls were precocious but others were cruelly slandered. In one particular year, several girls on the island, sixteen and under, were pregnant!

My sister, Mary An, would eventually have to run the gauntlet of young men, with whom she'd grown up as "playmates," but who would soon apply every pressure known to testosterone-fueled adolescent boys, to convert her into a playmate of another sort. My father decided it was more pressure than he, or Mary An, should endure.

* * *

That final boat ride from Peaks Island to the mainland landed us in a four-storied tenement on yet another hill--Monjoy Hill--in Portland. I'd never lived in a densely populated community before. The quieting effect of the ebb and flow of the tide was no longer audible from our new home. New sounds and smells triggered culture shock.

Tin cans, crushed to fit over one's shoes, allowed energetic wearers to run clickety-clackety up and down the sidewalk in the evening and became the replacement sound for the gentle carillon of channel buoys rocking in the currents. Mournful ships' whistles were replaced by ear shattering siren blasts. The sound of horse chestnuts thumping on our roof as sea breezes wrenched them loose from their stems were replaced by the sound of beer bottles smashing against alley walls.

Despite the loss of all that was familiar, I was still glad to be here. Dad's decision to move was also a relief to me. There were other aspects of island life I gladly left behind: One night, back in the early fifties, I took a shortcut home that ran along Cy Sennett's property. "Old Cy Sennett"—his name was always spoken with respect and admiration because he had returned from the war a decorated hero and retired as a high-ranking law enforcement officer.

Suddenly, out of the woods darted Matthew, a teenager who was generally recognized as "a bit different." He shoved me down, began ripping my clothes, grabbing me, and spewing threatening epithets that had yet to become part of my

11

vocabulary. My screaming and scratching combined with the difficulty of belts and button-flies, won out over the pervert's drive, and I was dismissed with a kick and a deadly threat. Frightened and humiliated, I kept the incident to myself. It strikes me as ironic that this assault took place in Cy's backyard, His Nibs being the retired Chief of Police and all. Several weeks later, while playing out on the point near Haddlock's Cove, a friend's older brother invited me into an old fishing shack he and his brothers had slapped together out of driftwood and tin. He was a familiar figure and I had no reason to be concerned about his intentions. Bad decision! Once inside the shack, I was threatened and forced to submit to the sexual abuse about which the "pasture pervert" had merely hinted. It was a big family—lots more guys where this one came from. I lived in mortal fear that his brother, who was my best friend, would find out about the incident. I knew I would never allow this to happen to me again, but lessons had been learned and damage done.

Another place where youngsters learn valuable lessons in life are in classrooms. Miss Brackett and Miss Thompson, the island's school marms, taught in the two-room schoolhouse long before I showed up. Although my creative mischief was not always appropriate, they remained caring and understanding. Life in the city school, however, was another story. I attended the Cathedral of the Immaculate Conception, a parochial school, run by the "Sisters of Mercy." I renamed it "The Cathedral of Amazing Misperceptions." Sisters of Mercy, indeed! I can't recall a single merciful one in the bunch, but that, no doubt, has more to do with my behavior than the sister's capacity for compassion.

On my way to school one day, a fat toad hopped out of Mrs. Mulcahey's garden. I scooped it up and slipped it into my pocket. Just how I would take advantage of this charming fellow had not yet jelled, but I sensed tremendous potential.

Perhaps a variation of Show-and-Tell might win some friends and influence a fair Colleen.

Each of our desks came equipped with its own ink well. Each student was issued a bottle of ink, one wooden stylus, and six nibs. I know, I know! What are nibs? Okay, nibs are the actual metal writing tips that once inserted into the stylus completes the "pen." The budding artist in me took control. I dipped the webbed feet of my warty accomplice into the inkwell and set him down on the white, Italian marble floor. Yes, indeed, he was quite a hit with the fairer sex!

Every morning a nun named Sister Mary Domitila, whom I quickly renamed Attila the Hun, would leave our classroom to attend a teachers' meeting where I assumed the "Merciful" devised a daily agenda of torment and torture for adolescent Irish/Italian angels. I was so enthralled with my newfound popularity that I failed to detect the clackety-clack of Attila's stubby-heeled shoes, until she was at the door. She reentered the room, and my toady teaching aid, who must have been saving himself for such an occasion, made a magnificent leap onto her shiny black shoe. Attila interpreted this as an assault upon her ankle.

I was sent to "the office," where I was introduced to the latest in state-of-the-art teaching tools. The function for which the pointer was purportedly designed would not be demonstrated in this session, but the function for which I am convinced the instrument was *really* designed became apparent. Twenty whacks across my palms reinforced a principle: I should be careful where I displayed my creative genius. Sisters of Mercy, 1; Mickey Farmer, 0.

My parent's move from the island to urban Portland, was prudent but life in the city would in time, ruin us all. It was either muster the will and determination to make a desperate break for freedom, or resign ourselves to the parade of programmed automatons plodding through the routine of city life. One year after our arrival in the world of tall buildings

13

and narrow sidewalks, Dad made the break and we settled in a handyman special in the "boonies."

*   *   *

There are no insights more powerful than a message from the grave. Not long after arriving in the country, a genuine friendship replaced the mobs of acquaintances, which substituted for friends in the city. I sensed I would survive. My new friend's name was Royal, and he lived in a farmhouse a mile away. One memorable wintry day, my dog and I set out to visit him via an old logging road that connected our properties.

Tiring of the monotony of trudging along the narrow path through the snow, my trusty canine companion, Mitty Bum, would periodically take off on small personal excursions only to rejoin me several hundred yards down the path. After an eighth of a mile of lonely trudging, I realized my faithful friend had abandoned me. Concerned, I followed his tracks and found myself in a pre-Civil War cemetery of the type common throughout the New England countryside.

The tracks led to a vault with a steel door sprung ajar by the frost heaves of winters past. The pooch was inside the vault, but immediately jumped out upon hearing my arrival. My imagination ran wild as I tried to see what the tomb contained. The reflection of sun on snow was so bright that I gave up—at least for the moment. That evening, under the guise of a before-bedtime-walk with Mitty Bum, I left the house. I had stashed a burlap sack and flashlight in the woodshed. We were off. Adrenaline replaced my blood as I approached the vault. As I swung the beam of light across the lintel of the vault, I read the large carved inscription, "CLEMENT." I climbed over the top of the mound, thrust my lower half through the crack, held on by my fingers, and dropped. I was in. Trusty Mitty Bum followed.

Gray slabs of slate formed honeycombs in the rear of the vault where skeletons lay feet first. The thrill of adventure overcame the fear of the dead. I gingerly pried Mr. Clement's head from his body and stuffed it in the sack. Only then did I give my first thought to getting out. Oops!

Mitty Bum leaped from the floor to the top of an urn and on through the opening. With less grace, but energized by sheer panic, I followed. Back on the logging road, I stopped for a drink of cold, fresh maple sap from a mason jar hanging from a spigot on a rock maple. In the jostling, ol' man Clement's jawbone came loose and fell unnoticed through a hole in the sack into the snow.

My return through the back door of my house was uneventful. No one noticed my burdened sack. My brother and I shared a bedroom but he was still in the living room listening to the radio so I pushed the grain sack under my bed, slid beneath the sheets, and pulled the blanket over my head.

Later that night, after the house was still, I shook my brother awake and began to tell him my story. Before I completed two sentences, he reached under my bed in disbelief and pulled out the sack. Onto the floor in full view rolled Mr. Clement's head! Dennis dived beneath his quilt and covered his head with pillows. No sooner had sleep overtaken him than a visitor arrived in my brother's dreams. The incomplete body of Mr. Clement was searching for fulfillment. Well, isn't everybody? My brother's screams were enough to curdle milk and the entire household was awakened. Parents have a way of cutting to the chase. "Where did this thing come from?"

I was ready. (I was always ready!) "Mom, do you remember those mounds where I was digging before the frost?"

From there it was easy. Mom had always been fascinated by American Indian culture. We were Irish, through and through, but mom has always laid claim to being part Indian. It's always puzzled me how two ethnic groups that have been historically held in such disdain have today become so stylish. Everyone wants to boast a "smattering," but not *too* much.

15

Of course, as with any plan there can be unexpected events. Mom insisted that I cart Chief Nobody to school where Mr. Schribner, the biology teacher, could authenticate him. He studied the skull, took some measurements, and proudly declared to the class, that it was from the hunter-gatherer tribe that wintered on the Standish Plains. (This guy's was a real scholar!) I may never have made the head of the class, but I could at least boast I'd brought one there! Excited by this latest bit of notoriety, Mr. Schribner placed a call to the *Portland Press Herald*.

This thing was getting way out of hand! I became an instant, albeit short-lived, celebrity. The front page of the *Herald* displayed a photo of me—shovel in hand—standing by the "burial mounds" at the end of our field. Anxiety began to set in when the misdiagnosed noggin got transferred to Dr. Bailey at the Gorham Normal School. A few days later, I was summoned to a solemn meeting where I discovered myself in the company of the local constable, my parents, and a Mrs. Hulda Irish, who lived on the farm across Route 25. This had not been a part of my plan.

It seems the man who tapped the maples and had provided the delicious drink after my grave-robbing debut, had found a human jawbone. Since he was not far from the cemetery, he figured a dog had taken it. Upon investigation he found the door ajar and discovered that the head to which the jaw belonged was also missing. It was too big of a task for a dog.

Hulda, it turns out, had a great uncle by the name of Alfred—one Alfred Clement, to be precise! Justice was swift and painful. Archeology would not be my forte, but new adventures were always just around the bend! I'd like to say that this fiasco concluded with my smoking the peace pipe, but the only smoke in sight was blowing out of my father's ears. This "brave" got restricted to the reservation!

*   *   *

Just as water seeks the path of least resistance, so does creativity. A person that concludes they are not especially acceptable to more responsible peers will predictably funnel creative juices toward gaining acceptance by others whose standards are not as high.

The group I linked up with in high school was quite creative. Although not popular with other students or teachers, my friends were in many respects more "genuine" than many of the guys from "better families." The camaraderie was wonderful. When we were not having massive amounts of fun, we were drinking and scheming, but this was a recipe for trouble and by my junior year, I was addicted.

When there were no dances or parties to amuse us, we carried out a series of B&Es (breaking and entering) on area businesses. My area of expertise was "casing the joint," (R & D for you corporate types). I didn't actually participate in the break-ins most of the time, but the few times I did nearly frightened me to death.

One incident in which I took part was at a large commercial battery store on a main street next to a railway crossing. After defeating the alarm system and entering through a rear window, we commenced to clean out drawers and cash registers. The store's plate glass windows faced the street, and while we were engrossed in gathering anything of value the entire showroom was flooded with light. There we stood, exposed like actors on a stage.

The intensity of the light grew rapidly, its origin revealed by an attention-arresting "ding-dong" and the screech of steel. A man in coveralls and railroad cap leaped down from the train and closed the bars backing up traffic. Anyone looking in our direction would have seen the only battery shop in the country with mannequins! We froze—literally held our breath—until the bars lifted and traffic moved away. It was over. The muscles in my neck ached from the tension.

17

The other crime in which I took an active part happened at the Paddock Diner across from the Gorham Raceway, a favorite haunt of local sulky drivers. Again, entry was made through a rear window at midnight. The local constable made his rounds here every other night and this should have been an off night. I hadn't yet learned to always expect the unexpected.

When we finished helping ourselves to cigarettes and money from the vending machines, we proceeded to the counter where the cash register was anchored. Bobby, one of my comrades-in-crime, discovered that the ancient stainless urn was still half full of hot coffee, and an apple pie whispered to us from the dessert rack. All jobs should come with a coffee break!

Deja vu! In the middle of our break, the plate glass window filled with headlights from the town cruiser, which had swung into a parking space in front of the restaurant. We ducked down and leaned our backs against the counter, but the mirrored wall behind us, now fully illuminated, revealed four young men huddled together, clear as a snapshot. The doorknob rattled. Satisfied that it was locked, the patrolman swung his flashlight in an arc across the counter. I looked up into the mirror and looked directly into his eyes. People don't see what they don't expect to see. We remained a "still life" of four frightened intruders, coffee in hand, while he stared through us. The cruiser door slammed and the bored patrolman went about his midnight routine.

Two of my three cohorts are either dead or doing life in prison. The other remains a chronic ne'er-do-well. They enjoyed committing crime; I participated for another reason. I couldn't--or didn't--see the healthier opportunities presented to me, so I created another kind of excitement, challenge, and adventure. There was something about being the ringleader and a part of a unit bound together by high-risk action that met a deeper need for security and significance.

18

My motivation, at that age to be accepted, is not unlike that which results in the proliferation of gangs today. It is important to separate the wrongdoing from creativity and channel the creativity into deeds worthy of commendation. If the more responsible and experienced among us overlook the opportunity to encourage the marginal members of the community, many will not be motivated to try harder. This latter group predictably makes everyone else's journey more painful and stressful.

*   *   *

Occasionally nature provides insight into our own human behavior. One such insight came years later as I drifted along the ocean shoreline in my Down East lobster boat. My attention was drawn to a huge nest of sticks and branches cradled in the first forks of an ancient oak tree. A female osprey was feeding her noisy offspring. The male flew close to the nest and as the full-sized hungry chick stretched over the edge of the nest toward a much anticipated meal, the mother unceremoniously forced her over the side. Merely inches from the roiling water and sharp rocks, the fledgling spread her wings and flew. Likewise, there comes that point in most people's lives when they are caught between the allure of adventure and leave-taking. The world draws like a magnet, but it sometimes takes a kick in the can to launch us out the door...

II. DESTINED FOR ANOTHER WORLD

It is encouraging to know that our course has been charted so each of us may reach our appointed destiny. Although situations may appear to be nothing more than luck or happenstance, they are pieces of the whole. Charts, warnings, and wise counsel are the tools by which we discover where our journey leads.

"Chief, this is my son and he's here to enlist." My dad had not sought my opinion on the matter. We had gone to Portland to pick up day-old bread at Nissens and sour milk at Hoods Dairy, which we used as pig feed. When we parked in front of the Post Office on India Street, I assumed it had to do with the mail. The fact that other government offices were located here meant nothing to me even though the sign over the door we were heading toward read, "United States Navy Recruiting Office." Two weeks later, I was being lulled to sleep by the clickety-clack of a Pullman flying over the rails en route to Great Lakes Naval Training Station, North Chicago--otherwise known as Boot Camp. Thus I was launched out of the nest into a whole other world.

The career that the navy had planned for me must have been an important task that involved a lot of standing in line because that is what I spent most of my waking hours doing! It was in one such line, waiting for uniform issue, that I met an elderly gentleman. He was obviously nonmilitary but was issuing little black books. This quiet old man's gift carried a powerful, time-released message that would one day, change my life.

"Yes, sir! Thank you, sir!" This military courtesy is reserved for authorities of rank. The military regulations didn't require it for this out-of-place old veteran, but time would reveal just how appropriate my response was.

What was I supposed to do with a Protestant New Testament? It rapidly found its way to the very bottom of my sea bag where it would wait for another day--another story.

"Stanley M. Farmer—Fireman Apprentice." Names representing every ethnic group rang out, but they were all background noise until I heard my own. The yeoman handed my orders to me and I was on my way to the U.S. Submarine Base, Groton, Connecticut. This, in itself, was considered an accomplishment, but before I could be considered submarine material I had to complete the 100-foot underwater ascent.

22

I still recall that day in 1961. The surface appeared as a lens in a spyglass, just beyond my reach. My lungs felt as if they were on fire, and ready to burst. I remembered my training and forced myself to continue blowing air out of my lungs. "Where was all this air coming from?" I thought, "When will I be able to inhale?" Bursting through the lens into an oxygen-rich atmosphere was an experience I imagine to be like leaving earth and entering heaven. The next best thing, maybe! Arriving at the surface alive meant that I was qualified to serve aboard the USS SARDA-SS 488, a W.W. II Fleet Class submarine operating as a school boat out of New London.

Learning how to operate the critical systems aboard the old diesel sub occupied every hour during my first six months aboard that I was not actually standing watch or sleeping. Veteran submariners observed the rookies as we demonstrated that we could perform each vital task. Upon successful passage of these tests and drills, I was awarded my "dolphins"--a silver pin depicting a head-on view of a Fleet submarine being escorted by a pair of dolphins. This insignia is evidence that the wearer is "Qualified in Submarines" and cherished by its wearer more than any medal or promotion.

The evening after the Captain pinned the dolphins on me the Young Men's Christian Association (WMCA) sponsored a dance for servicemen stationed in the Groton/New London area. As I returned to the SARDA following a wonderful evening, I told my shipmate, Jim Waldrop, that Joan, the girl with whom I had danced most of the evening, had agreed to see me again. To my surprise, Jim begged me not to pursue her. He felt she was too nice a girl for me. Some friend! But I was hooked.

Six months later the Waterford Drive-in was showing "Lady Chatterley's Lover," but Joan and I never saw the movie. Joan knew I had invited her there for reasons other than the movie, because the screen was not visible for the dense pea soup fog that New England is famous for. I proposed, and three months later we were married. Joan's dad, a British-born Protestant cop, didn't approve of his "baby" marrying a common sailor. If that were not bad enough, my mother, in all seriousness, sent my wife-to-be a Sympathy Mass card--intended for the bereaved!

Soon after our wedding, it became apparent to Joan that I had a serious problem with alcohol. Being married and in love didn't erase the painful and destructive images from my own upbringing. One image freeze-framed in my memory bank held a boy sitting in the pouring rain on an abandoned car seat with his unconscious, drunken dad. The next frame showed the boy helping his dad to his feet after he had stumbled from a friend's old Studebaker into a mud puddle.

When Dad was not drinking, which was most of the time, he was the best dad anyone could have. There ought to be a warning label on liquor bottles warning users of its ability to completely alter ones personality. Despite the good times, my mind replayed the hundreds of hours of bitter fighting between my parents. As this dream began to play out in real time, I swore never to embarrass my own children that way. But by age twenty-one, I was becoming a carbon copy of my dad--compulsive, angry, and suicidal. It was into this environment that my son, Shawn, was born.

Prior to my assignment to the USS SARDA, I had been accepted to Admiral Rickover's Nuclear Power Academy. After several months, I was given an academic drop. In truth, my drinking was catching up with me and I was not able to keep up with my studies. When you flunked out of "Nuke School" you were sent to the Fleet, which was a submariners' equivalent of Siberia. If the USS SARDA (SS-488) was Rickover's idea of Siberia, it was my Riviera—I loved it!

About a year after I'd come aboard, the yeoman called me into the ship's office. There were orders for me to return to

Nuclear Power Academy. Unheard of! You never got a second chance to attend this elite course. As soon as I entered the Academy, I was directed to Captain Carnihan's office. The words from this white-haired mustang Captain had a familiar ring. The voice was not a rich baritone, like that of my high school principal, yet the words were equally encouraging.

"Young man, I hear you got married last year?"

"Yes, sir, Captain!" "You have become a father, I see?"

"Yes sir, Captain!"

"I have looked at your record and have spoken with the skipper aboard SARDA. He says you've got what it takes. If I see you in this office before graduation, I'll bust you to Seaman Recruit and you and your new little family will be on welfare! Do you understand me, sailor?"

"Yes, sir, Captain!" It worked!

*   *   *

Nuclear physics, heat transfer and fluid flow--new subjects all--created plenty of stress, but it was a cadre of overly zealous young Christians carrying large, black Bibles, apparently co-written by some long since deceased King of England and one Mr. Scoffield. They would congregate in the barracks and on high grassy spots outside and sing corny songs while faithful helpers handed out wretched pamphlets that grated me even more. Terry, their unofficial spokesman, was known for inflammatory outbursts such as "all you Catholics are going to hell!" "The Pope is the Anti-Christ!" It seemed to me that immigrant stock from the south of Ireland might be particularly threatened. Looking back, I realize that Terry was filled with the passion of one with newfound faith but with little maturity to temper the zeal. At that moment however, I thought, *This guy had better be in good standing with his own Maker!*

I looked forward to graduating from Nuclear Power Academy as much to be rid of these kooks as to getting on with my career. Graduation finally came, and I was selected to attend Advanced Nuclear Power School at Bettis Laboratories in Pittsburgh, Pennsylvania. The class of thirty-two men included me and, you guessed it, the ringleader of the religious zealots.

Military personnel were required to dress and behave as civilians in the university setting and to find accommodations like the other engineering students. No provision was made for wives to join their husbands so Joan, pregnant with our second child, remained in Connecticut.

"Stan, the Red Cross has been trying to get hold of you all weekend--something about your wife's pregnancy." A baby had been born, a girl, but she was hanging on by a thread. Joan was very weak and the situation was critical. Papers in order, I sped toward Connecticut.

An hour outside of Pittsburgh, the strobe of blue lights illuminated my rearview mirror. After receiving a speeding ticket, an encounter with a very manly Ms. Justice of the Peace, and encouragement from a sympathetic Pennsylvania State Trooper, I was back on the road--sixty dollars poorer but with whispered clearance to speed to the New Jersey state line.

Five hours later, I entered Lawrence and Memorial Hospital in New London to encounter my heartbroken wife. Our much-anticipated daughter, Dawn Michelle, had been taken to heaven. There is no way I can pretend to comprehend the misery and pain the loss of a child brings to a mother, but I had longed for a daughter and also felt the loss. Life would go on, but it would be forever altered by her death.

Following another graduation, I was assigned to the USS Ulysses Grant—SSBN 631 that was yet to be built at the General Dynamics Electric Boat plant in Groton, Connecticut. With more than sixty crews to be filled and only thirty-three nuclear graduates available, what would be the chances of ending up trapped aboard a double-ended steel cigar with "you-know-who?" You guessed it! I couldn't get rid of this guy.

26

This turned out to be a really great assignment because Joan's family lived in nearby Niantic, Connecticut. In the aftermath of our great loss, my personal behavior went downhill. Instead of remaining strong for Joan, I turned to the bottle. Alcohol again became a major factor in my life. On one occasion a shipmate carefully suggested that if I didn't get hold of myself soon, I would be kicked out of submarines--and possibly out of the Navy.

It was dawning on me that Joan would not--and most certainly should not--endure the insecurity and verbal abuse much longer. I was vomiting blood on Monday mornings and my weekend behavior was jeopardizing our marriage. Unbeknownst to me our son Shawn, now three years old, absorbed every fight, every shed tear, and the palpable tension present in our home.

Ever since the USS GRANT began sea trials Terry, my "religious friend," had been slipping me small cards with Scripture written on them. His demeanor had changed and a more loving, caring person had emerged. He started telling me about God and I began to listen, which brought back some distinct, albeit confusing memories.

One of my very early attempts to figure out where God might reside came about in our home during a very confusing incident. The bathroom was occupied and my father was pacing around very worked up over something. As I have said, my father wasn't around enough to say much of anything, so when he did speak I had the tendency to take notice. Dad stormed up to the bathroom door and pounded on it, swearing loudly, "God, are you still in there?" Only later would I realize that Dad was delivering the punch line of an age-old joke. Until a moment before, I had thought that my brother was the bathroom's most recent occupant. This outburst raised some serious questions in my mind!

27

During the years I served as an altar boy and attended Catholic school, I received more profound training about religion. I discovered that God was, in fact, not in the bathroom, but locked in a box on top of the altar. There, He was flattened out into a disk that looked like a Necco wafer. Having been taught that this was where God *really* dwelt, I concluded that if I were God, I would rather be confined to the bathroom!

Another early impression of God and religious people occurred when I came home from school one day and discovered the parish priest--an old, bald-headed fellow named Father Sullivan--standing over an ironing board with a steam iron in hand pressing a shirt. My mother was nowhere around but the house was open. (The fact that the house was left unlocked was not unusual. Not a house on the island had a lock on the door--that would be absurd, and a waste of money, not to mention an insult to your neighbor!)

I asked the "Father" if he knew where my mother was and he said, "Yes, I think she's down at Tuttles." In order to preserve their sanity, island women often ventured out during the afternoons to visit a neighbor. Mrs. Tuttle was a matriarch with thirteen (or was it fifteen?) children. My dad always maintained that old Eddie Tuttle wasn't so much Catholic as he was careless!

When Father Sullivan came to visit our house and found the ironing board set up with no one home, he simply did what needed to be done and finished ironing the few shirts that had been freshly sprinkled. This encounter with a "minister" has always helped me keep a balanced perception of what men of God ought to be about.

* * *

Terry talked to me about God but his picture contrasted with mine. When I would tolerate it, he would tell me that I was too important to God to ruin my life as I was doing and that God really did love me. He said that if I would accept God's love, God would forgive my sin and heal my heart.

My heart was sick. I was sick. I knew I would lose my wife and son. It was decision time. I was at a fork in the road, a point of major personal choice. It was here that my adventure would really begin.

I was on watch in the Lower Level Auxiliary Machinery Room #2. From this station the bubble was drawn in the reactor allowing it to go critical. As I reflected on the state of my life a sense of grief overcame me. I asked to be relieved to go to the "head," but instead continued on to the Forward Torpedo Room where my bunk lay outboard a live "fish,"--the submariner's name for an armed torpedo. Under the flashcover of my mattress a seabag lay flattened out. At the very bottom of the bag was the little black book I had received in boot camp. I thought of the Gideon Testament, because it was small enough to be tucked inside my shirt under my belt. I was too ashamed to be seen carrying a Protestant Bible--how pathetic!

Once back on watch, I took a round of temperature and pressure readings and was free to open the book and look up the verses that Terry had written on index cards. It was there, four hundred feet under the Atlantic Ocean, somewhere near Bermuda, that I surrendered my sorry butt to Jesus. That simple act would mark a U-turn on a dead-end road and the beginning of a wonderful adventure. I had made the right choice. I was now heading in the right direction. The journey was on!

I'd like to say that drinking immediately became a thing of the past, but this was not the case. It did begin to decrease, however, and there were radical changes in my language and my attitude toward Joan and Shawn. I did not know where it would lead, but new "stuff" was starting. The Bible became the most exciting book I'd ever read. I spent every spare moment studying or talking about it with the growing nucleus of like-minded men, who, up until now, I had failed to notice.

Inspection and tests completed, the USS ULYSSES GRANT SSBN 631 was accepted by the Navy and proceeded through the Panama Canal to her new home-- "Aloha!" After a warm reception in Hawaii, the GRANT steamed to her permanent station in Guam. I was now spending more than half of my life beneath the ocean. Joan and our son Shawn were living in a bungalow on the backside of the island of Oahu, left alone with no relatives or friends.

Wives were left to the morbid sense of dread that has always been associated with men at war or at sea, haunted by the rumors always circulating and by the nightmares their men experienced when they returned home. Life consisted largely of waiting for their husbands to return. The Vietnam conflict had erupted with a vengeance. Our neighbors' husbands--marines from Kaneoee--left for work one morning as usual and didn't return that night. Their wives had not been forewarned! Most never returned.

When a submarine surfaces after being submerged for months, the first item every sailor clamors for is mail. Literally tons of mail awaits a submarine's return. After my second extended patrol, I was surprised to discover that Joan had written to me nearly every day. Her letters were filled with talk about God. It was clear something wonderful had happened.

As it turned out, Joan had been attending a woman's Bible study at a church in Pearl City. During my patrol, she made a commitment to follow Jesus. I chose to be submerged in a different way soon after arriving back in Honolulu, and this time Joan was submerged with me. We were baptized together at a local church.

The loss of baby Dawn now sufficiently distant, Joan and I yearned for another child--not a replacement, but an additional son or daughter to raise with Shawn. Shawn's birth had stimulated a strong antibody reaction to a severe Rh factor that had attacked baby Dawn. This condition is now easily defeated by a treatment known as RhoGAM. It was not available in the early sixties and conceiving could have been fatal to Joan. We decided to adopt but were told that with only a year and a half left on my enlistment, it would be impossible to adopt in Hawaii. We could try anyway, and we did.

A son or daughter would do, but I privately prayed for a daughter. Every dad ought to have one! Our prayer was answered and we were notified that a baby awaited us at Princess Lilliukelani Hospital. Joan and I were introduced to the most beautiful brown-eyed, brown-haired baby that God ever created! I've received few greater gifts in my lifetime than Sherree. Holding her, I was aware that God had a plan. It was a miracle that she was ours. "Ask no questions," we were told when I inquired of the social worker as to how this could have happened.

God had been doing wonderful "stuff" in our lives, but this tangible gift overwhelmed us. We were convinced Sherree was a gift from God. But if this were just the beginning of our adventure, what would be in store for the rest of our journey?

III. ADVENTURE BECKONS

The most exciting junkets are originals. For many, the hardest part of a journey is the decision to leave the familiar. Fear of the unknown can be a powerful deterrent to adventure, but it is the unknown that has the potential to reveal secrets and unravel the mysteries that bring excitement to one's life. Listen carefully for an invitation to begin a new adventure. It may come from a most unlikely source.

One day I decided to go fishing with my buddy Tracy, a lad whose courage and lack of common sense matched my own. The whole bay was literally filled with schools of mackerel and squid, and the watermelon-fishy smell, peculiar to large schools of fish on the surface, filled the air.

Tracy and I grabbed our hand lines and ran down to the dock and proceeded to catch mackerel by the hundreds. We slathered broom handles with lard and stuck them into the water. When the squid wrapped themselves around the greased poles, we jerked them out, ink spraying everywhere. They would end up as fertilizer in our gardens.

This successful fishing bonanza filled the morning with excitement, but fulfilling as this activity may seem, it takes quite a lot to keep two adolescent hooligans focused for very long. The antenna began scanning for a higher level of stimulation, and we were soon rewarded. It is apparent that "Mother Nature" is as anxious to provide eleven- and twelve-year-old lads with variety and diversion as the lads are to have it.

By afternoon, several pods of full-grown porpoises came roaring into the bay gorging themselves on the mackerel and squid. These playful creatures kept rolling to the surface—bidding us to play. I thought, *this is excitement!* Tracy and I made a hasty executive decision to swipe a punt from the camel next to the pier and head out to join the fun.

I'll bet you didn't think we had camels on islands off the coast of Maine! Let me explain: Our "camel" is a heavy wooden raft secured to the edge of a pier by lines; it allows small boats access to the pier when the tide rises and falls the expected ten or eleven feet during the course of six hours. A "punt" is an eight-foot wooden rowboat with a flat bottom, blunt stern, pointed bow, and a sculling groove in the transom which allows those adequately skilled, to propel it with a single oar. The local lobstermen use punts as mooring tenders and work skiffs.

After an uncharacteristic pang of conscience, I concluded that borrowing the punt without asking was no big deal. When a punt was not being used the fishermen really didn't mind them being taken for a short time. (At least that was true for island-raised kids of our day.)

Tracy and I sculled into the vast school of fish where the porpoises were in a feeding frenzy. Each mammal ranged from fifty to two hundred pounds. I had not yet been introduced to life jackets. In fact, "safety" was not in my vocabulary nor was it a concept I had thought much about at that point in my life. In my world, you learned to swim at an early age or you were in real trouble.

When the porpoises rolled up to rub and jostle the boat, it raised the level of excitement to new heights. This was great fun. We were having the adventure of a lifetime--the adrenaline was threatening to sink the punt. During this natural high, we decided to expand our horizons. We each took off a sneaker, held it by the toe, and thumped these ocean-bound beasties on their backs as they rolled up. It seemed to us that they were enjoying the game as much as we were.

Tracy's mom, as it happened, had been alerted that her son and the terrible miscreant, "Mickey Farmer," were out in a stolen punt, risking their lives chasing after visiting leviathans. Over our squeals of excitement we began to hear Tracy's mother screaming at the top of her lungs. Tracy glanced toward the shore and was momentarily distracted by what looked like a goose valiantly trying to take flight from the wharf, but clearer focus revealed Tracy's mom frantically waving her arms. Paralyzed with fear, Tracy let his sneaker slip from his grip. I am still convinced that one of those porpoises snagged his sneaker and swam off with it. If you should ever see King Neptune standing in the seaweed wearing one sneaker, it's probably Tracy's!

With our mother-to-child shriek detection system on full alert, we headed for shore as fast as we could. Had we known what awaited us we might have taken our time. Back on land the remaining sneaker was no threat to the porpoises, but it left definite tread-marks on our smooth, pink, derrieres!

The thrill and excitement of that day remain vivid. However, the painful correction I received taught me that not everyone involved in my life would necessarily be amused by my adventures.

*   *   *

Many years later, as I looked out to sea from a cafe on the beach at Waikiki, my mind returned to the rugged coast of Maine. As I reminisced about my adventures there, I wondered what exciting adventures awaited me following the end of my enlistment. At just that moment two men approached my table interrupting my thoughts. They had the look of "government types." In a world of short-sleeved tourists and military uniforms, these guys stood out like doughnut venders at a Weight Watcher's convention. They were, in fact, citizens of a foreign country--Australia--but not government agents. (Submariners were advised daily to be aware of agents of foreign governments who, under some pretense, were stationed in Oahu. They hung out in bars, on the beach, and in hotels, hoping to compromise servicemen who worked in "classified environments," of which Hawaii had many.) The Aussies, however, were legit. They wanted to hire me as a supervisor at the proposed nuclear station in New South Wales, Australia, after my discharge. I had become sufficiently disenchanted with my nation's activities in Vietnam, that Joan and I decided we would accept this new challenge.

As my enlistment expiration date rolled around, the Navy extended my enlistment for reasons of "national security." They spent six months attempting to convince me to wear Lieutenant, Junior Grade (JG) bars as an engineer on a Mekong River gunboat. They must have thought my mother had raised a parcel of idiots! Sensing their attempt to add my name to a yet-to-be-built wall on the Washington Mall, I declined. Instead, I was assigned to an intelligence-gathering submarine USS BARBEL, SS-580 currently operating places in Asia where U. S. Forces were neither welcome nor authorized. As it turned out fighting in Vietnam's Mekong Delta swamps may have posed less risk! The life-threatening experiences aboard the Barbel, (documented in the best-selling book, *Blind Man's Bluff* by Sherry Sontag, published in 1999), did little to change my mind about returning to civilian life.

As I was being separated from the service at Treasure Island, California. Word arrived that my dad had suffered a massive heart attack and might not live. We packed up everything we owned and drove our little Opel Rekord back East. The trip exhausted our financial reserves and dictated the decision as to where we would begin civilian life. We would settle in New England.

After a five-day drive across the country, we arrived in the little Maine community that I had left eight years before. It was with a certain anxiousness and delight that I pulled into a gas station owned by a local old-timer. He knew my family and had known me all through high school. I wondered how he would respond to seeing me after all these years. It was raining pretty hard, but he stopped to study the license plate--"Hawaii."

"Fill 'er up, Fred," I said, which he did without comment. I handed him my credit card and he carried it off to the shop. Still no comment.

Soon he returned, handed it back, and without so much as a trace of emotion or recognition, looked me in the eye and said, "Must a' been a wet drive, wont'it?" I was back home!

* * *

My nuclear experience landed me the position of Health Physicist at a nuclear power station under construction at Haddam, Connecticut. In the following year, I unionized the plant, organizing a local chapter of the IBEW (International Brotherhood of Electrical Workers), and became the union's first business manager. This paved the way to a new job selling radiation detection equipment for an electronics firm. The surest way I know to get promoted to management or be shown the door of opportunity is to organize a labor union!

As sales and marketing manager for Eberline Instruments, I could choose where to live and opted for Coeyman's Hollow, New York. We invested all of our savings in a one-hundred-year-old, historic Federal in the village. A small Pentecostal church nearby had recently called a pastor to serve them. He was a Jewish convert to Christianity and had grown up in affluent Long Island, New York. His orthodox family had disowned him for his change of faith, and, as a result, the young seminarian found himself trying to support his wife and children on the meager salary offered by the church. Joan and I learned of this and although it was not the church we attended, we decided to rent the second floor of our house to the Rosens.

Shortly after settling in the Catskil community, Joan's dad's health began to fail. We wanted to be closer to her family in Connecticut and so once again we changed our course. This meant selling the wonderful Federal. Seldom do I succumb to huge unselfish sacrificial urges, but at that time I did.

"Mr. Rosen," I said, "I'm selling the house, would you like to buy it?"

Rosen was visibly shaken. The prospect of locating another apartment was frightening and I could see the disappointment all over his face. "I am in no position to purchase anything," he finally replied.

"Are you able to make your monthly payments?" Of course he could. He had been making them all along. "Then keep making them. Just make them to the bank, and I'll contribute our equity."

Now there was the deal of a lifetime! The Rosens had a home they didn't expect to have, and we were free to move to Connecticut--minus the equity we had invested. We left New York and rented a small Cape in the shoreline town of Niantic, Connecticut where we could be of assistance to Joan's mom and failing dad.

Soon we were introduced to a thriving church in Groton, Connecticut, and we became active members. Life was good. I was respected in the community as a businessman and in the church as a young "up-and-comer." I enjoyed a liberal expense account and Joan frequented her favorite clothing stores with regularity. Shawn and Sherree were fully engaged in the activities of a great local school. It was time to settle into a comfortable secure life-style. I had no idea that a new adventure was nearly upon us.

Little did I realize that the road was being paved before me. One day the pastor and one of the long-term members of the church invited me to a meeting of New England church leaders representing our "non-denomination" denomination. I was flattered and considered it a privilege.

On the way home, as I sat in the back seat of the station wagon, I overheard the driver saying, "What our area needs is a Christian bookstore. There is not a single Christian bookstore in Eastern Connecticut." My decision was essentially made there on the spot. This was clear to me by the way the idea began to ferment in my mind. I was already believing it and visualizing the reality. Books! I loved books. This was going to be a blast!

*　　*　　*

In 1969 Joan and I opened Bread of Life Bookstore on Bridge Street in Groton. This seemingly benign venture had a major impact on our lives and the lives of many others. It played a crucial role in the eventual birth of His Mansion, a ministry to troubled young adults. My experiences in operating the store greatly expanded my knowledge of the many organizations and various methods used in proclaiming God's message to the world. Virtually every variety of Christian walked through those doors and many of them left a lasting impression on me.

One day, during a slow morning, a portly senior citizen came in alone. She had been to a revival conference and had gained fresh insights and "spiritual gifts." Immediately she noticed that one of my legs was shorter than the other leg (a problem that had eluded me for twenty-eight years). She asked if I would place my foot on the counter so she could right the matter.

Being concerned--after all, the lady had admitted to being a novice at the procedure--I inquired as to how we might proceed if, after the happening, the shorter turned out the longer. Discouraged by my spiritual backwardness, she abandoned the project and left, much to my relief.

The store was the hub of great activity. Some days it resembled a Catholic confessional booth and at other times great theological debates roared like a bonfire. The excitement of new experiences in the store overflowed into our home. Just as I was drawn to race out into the bay where the porpoises were frolicking, I plunged into this new adventure, taking in the thrill of every pitch and roll.

The Bread of Life Bookstore was a money loser from the start, so I contracted out as a consultant to the nuclear industry one week out of each month. Calling on nuclear related industries in the Northeast incurred a lot of driving and consequently, I picked up hitchhikers as much to war against boredom as to learn firsthand what made this strange new generation tick. This really worked well for me because I was, in fact, deeply concerned with the changes I sensed in the young adult culture around me and was certain that some sort of supernatural phenomena was at the core. No other situation in my life would have afforded me this unique opportunity. I had concluded that the solution must be of a spiritual nature and that I needed to better understand how it all worked. This could be accomplished by reading everything other people thought or by interviewing those actually experiencing the lifestyle. On rare occasions one of my late-night pickups would end up spending the night at our house.

On one such night toward the end of the sixties, I rescued a little band of five hippies on the highway, brought them home, and made them at home on our living room floor. When everyone seemed settled in, I quietly slipped into bed with Joan and quickly fell asleep. In several short hours the morning light began to fill the room. Groans and stretches signaled the awakening of my tribe. When Joan experienced her daily resurrection and appeared reasonably coherent, I asked her if she remembered the scripture passage that spoke about people entertaining angels unaware. Being a very quick study and because I have established a reputation for such foolishness, Joan immediately asked what kind of company I was talking about. I informed her that they were already in the living room!

When my bride, the mother of two young children, peeked into the living room, there were five people (three sleeping bags!?) scattered about the floor. The smell of stale pot smoke was heavy in their clothing. After they stirred, we fed them and sent them on their way. My family became used to surprises like this and our children found such visitors quite interesting.

I was very curious about "acid trips" and "flashbacks," as this was the stuff of daily grist in the media. There were stories on the nightly news of young adults going crazy, jumping out windows, attempting to fly, hearing strange voices, etc.

41

The media also seemed preoccupied with Satanic ritual abuse (SRA), and other supernatural phenomena. I seldom missed any opportunity to grill young prospects concerning their personal experiences, where they were heading, and why. Several suspected that I was a "NARC" or some kind of shrink.

It intrigued me that so many of the traveling hippies related stories of drug experiences that were sinister--and similar--in detail. The hitchhikers I picked up came from the four corners of the United States and could not possibly have met to get their stories straight. They would have had little interest in reading the same books or agreeing on a common fantasy anyway.

The stories that intrigued me most had to do with "out-of-body" experiences and "other dimensional" stuff. Many of my riders readily admitted to using hallucinogens such as LSD, mushrooms, and other types of mind-altering substances. Nearly all were quite willing to describe what they saw and experienced under the influence of chemicals. Many seemed preoccupied with what they called, their "bad trips." You would think they had rehearsed lines from a shared script!

The scenario was typical: A bunch of folks would get together to smoke reefer, drink wine, and progressing to "hits" of acid. It was the stuff of the Timothy Leary cult. Soon their perception would be altered. Their five senses interchanged, leading to *tasting* music, *hearing* tears, *smelling* colors, all providing fresh "insight" into reality. Fragments of conversations, broadcast news, and newspaper articles were absorbed and reconstructed into "messages" that warned of communist attacks and sinister conspiracies.

Quite frequently, during a drug-induced state, the individuals experienced the phenomenon of rising out of themselves and hovering over their bodies. In fact, this was often the intended experience--the goal of getting high. Many would go on to repeat this experience over and over, each time perceiving themselves to have moved farther away from their bodies and "staying out" longer. It was during one of these out-of-body experiences that problems often occurred.

After the separation of their "souls" from their bodies, many experimenters "freaked out" and reacted with appropriate fear, panic shocking them back into reality. Others were enamored enough to continue venturing into the "other world." A significant number of those broke loose and never came back. They are still in mental institutions or prisons, or pushing shopping carts around inner cities.

Many of my passengers related their bad trips to me as we drove along the Interstate. Bad trips were usually comprised of the same basic ingredients, but the things they encountered while outside of themselves were of particular interest to me. Those under the influence of mind-altering chemicals testified to seeing demonic-looking "beings," that are not visible to the rest of us. They described it as "stepping into another dimension." Indeed! I believe that is exactly what they were doing, or where they were going.

* * *

Not all of my adventures were with certified aliens, however. Joan and I were asked to lead an activity group for senior high and college-aged young folks at our church and although they certainly were different, they were not quite aliens. The group met in our home because this was the era when young people were anti-parent, antipolice, antimilitary, anti-teacher, and especially antichurch. They *were* quite fond of themselves, however.

On Friday nights our place was hopping with ping-pong, food, and discussions. This group of darlings was getting to me. They put their feet up on the furniture, ate everything in sight, wore no underclothing, avoided taking showers, and seldom said "thank you." I wanted out of the commitment almost as soon as we accepted it.

43

One Friday night the group discussion evolved around some "hard-to-believe" miracles, notably the story of Jesus raising Lazarus from the dead. As we read through this and prepared to talk it over, we read the part where Jesus turned to the folks who professed to love Lazarus and challenged them to begin to unwrap the decayed body. When I read the verse that describes Jesus asking those who professed to love Lazarus to reach out and touch him--unwrap him, I was personally humbled and felt a deep sense of hypocrisy and guilt for my attitude toward these young adults. But as is often true, it took more than just cognitive recognition and personal remorse for me to act differently. Reality therapy came a few mornings later when Lazarus showed up in our living room!

*   *   *

In the predawn hours, the doorbell shattered my early morning sleep. It was Mike, a young man who had been attending the Friday night Bible study. He stood there in anguish, his wife of several weeks limp in his arms. This was not a gallant groom carrying his maid over the threshold. Alicia, Mike announced, was dead!

We placed Alicia on the couch. My first order of business was *not* to awaken Joan and get her involved. No such luck! Dead folks, although quiet, are very difficult to hide in a small house on short notice. Joan, curious about the commotion, came into the living room and discovered my emotional friend and his not-so-emotional wife.

Joan first ensured that our two living children did not wake up and have to see their first dead guest. She succeeded where I had failed and the business at hand could now be addressed. What exactly do you do with a dead person and her grieving husband?

In times of crisis involving sickness or physical accidents, I pray--and then call the doctor!

44

Did I know any doctors? It was five o'clock in the morning! Ah, yes, "Doctor" Jessiman. Well, Ed was a psychologist with a Ph.D., but a doctor nonetheless! The chances of Ed being home at 5:00a.m. on Memorial Day were good. Voila! He was there and offered great advice.

After hearing the details of Alicia's demise, Dr. Ed considered the possibility that she might still be alive. (Good thing I hadn't decided on an impromptu burial!) At his coaching, I heated a needle and poked Alicia in various locations to discover that my Lazarus was not dead. Instead, she was comatose from a heroin overdose and in a few hours Alicia regained consciousness. She remained in our home for several weeks, then returned to her parents' home in western Connecticut.

A week after Alicia left, the clerk at Bread of Life Bookstore called to tell me he could not open the shop due to the presence of a body against the door, apparently dead. My recent experience told me that this could also be a diagnosis drawn too hastily. Much to my relief, the young man was not dead. He had been directed by Alicia to seek out the "Farmers" at their bookstore because she had forgotten our home address.

Our new doorstop's name was Rick, and he also recuperated from a heroin overdose at our home. One morning, as Rick and the Farmer family ate breakfast, we heard a distinct "clink" in Rick's cereal bowl. His front tooth had fallen out into his breakfast! Heroin has a tendency to rob the body of calcium and weaken teeth. He looked up with a silly grin to display a huge gaping hole in his mouth. Shawn and Sherree were caught between laughing and crying. No school-based, drug awareness class could match the impression events such as this has made upon them.

Rick was then followed by "Fast Eddie," and for the next year there was always someone living in our attic. As a result of the insight gained from these experiences, it became apparent to me just how devastating this new wave of drug use would be to our culture and families. The tide was changing and I would soon be swept into a new adventure by it.

*   *   *

During the late sixties the highways, town greens, and public parks were crowded with restless, rebellious, joy-seeking youths. Many were following the lead of rock star idols and older high-profile dissidents. LSD, pot, and alcohol became the elements of daily communion for the culture's faithful adherents. Flower children, hippies, freaks—they came with all sorts of labels, wearing every imaginable costume--could be found hitchhiking in crisscross patterns across the country. Rockfests, protests, and flying saucer sightings--any excuse was reason enough to set out on a journey and get high.

Toward the end of this era, great numbers of these "wanderers" made decisions to follow Jesus Christ. Having tried sex, drugs, rock 'n roll, and every other faddish cult that emerged during those years, these people were searching for meaning. Although eastern mysticism was making major inroads among those who had become disillusioned with the drug culture, it was Christianity that proved to be truly life transforming.

The resulting influx of highly motivated, uninitiated zealots created a dilemma for the church. This army of converts known as "Jesus freaks," filled the back rows of sanctuaries and frightened the daylights out of elders, deacons, and other church powerbrokers. These newcomers spoke a different language, wore ratty clothing (certainly not enough), took infrequent baths, didn't shave anything, and wanted answers to a hundred questions. Having had little indoctrination into the many rituals practiced in our churches, they demanded "reality." Pastors and parents alike were often intimidated and reacted out of fear, labeling the "Jesus freaks" as rebels and troublemakers.

In spite of the bad rap they received, they grew in the knowledge of God and were as ready to follow Jesus as were the early disciples. From this movement has come the vast majority of today's "movers-and-shakers" in cutting-edge churches, mission agencies, Christian educational institutions, and parachurch ministries. In fact, the "Jesus People" movement has been the most significant force in Christian culture during the last half of the nineteenth century.

I saw the thousands of frightened and discouraged victims of the free-love, mind-bending counterculture as a huge pool of potential. Yes, they were in sad shape. Yes, they needed love and compassion. But if they could be restored, they would restore others in turn. I became convinced that I needed to be involved in this process.

My over-the-counter conversations with patrons at the bookstore showed me there were others who recognized that our culture was fertile soil in which the seeds of moral and civil breakdown would germinate, contaminating an entire generation of teens and young adults. Some of those folks were taking this challenge personally. One such person was Hal Moore, the Officer-in-Charge of the New London Laboratory of the US Naval Underwater Systems Center in New London. Hal volunteered at Altruism House, a secular drug treatment facility. There he and his wife Mary, developed a special relationship with a troubled young woman in the program. Their attempts to introduce God's plan for healing were not well received but Hal was determined. He visited the bookstore often seeking new resources that might help those he did get to interact with. Joan and I were also dealing with addicts so a friendship quickly formed around our common burden.

There was another man, Joe Wagner, who had become like a father to me, and who shared our concern for salvaging young lives ravaged by drugs and alcohol. Together, Joe and I had already intervened in the lives of dozens of confused and broken young men and women. I sensed it was time for the three of us--Hal, Joe, and me--to meet. We met at Hal's house to discuss the need we knew existed. After a time of prayer we decided God would have us begin the ministry that soon became His Mansion. On that evening, December of 1971, God spoke. Okay, I don't know exactly *how* He did it, but make no mistake about it--God spoke.

Just as surely as Tracy and I had responded to his mother's voice across the water as we chased porpoises around the bay, Joe, Hal, and I heard God's voice that night and we took action. God would have us organize a board and start a program for addicts. That this vision would come to be, there was absolutely no doubt. Although this has not been the typical way God has dealt with me, it was so real that it never occurred to me to question it. For Hal, who was much newer in his faith experience, this meeting has left its mark as a special moment of faith. Joe and I were no less moved and thus God had set in motion an adventure far greater than the three of us envisioned at the time.

IV. LEAVING FAMILIAR TERRITORY

There comes a point in most endeavors when you arrive at the borders of all that is comfortable, familiar, and predictable. To continue is to enter an unknown world. The risks are obvious, but there are also rewards. You can stay put and be secure, or step out and "see." First steps require faith, but faith that has reason to trust is not blind.

Saturday mornings, during my boyhood island years, would occasionally offer an opportunity to escape to the mainland to help my mom do the weekly shopping and to visit relatives. During winter months all the passengers on the ferry would be familiar island folk, but during the summer I would be assured of seeing and meeting people from "away."

The socioeconomic contrast between the year-round residents and the army of summer immigrants was vast. The Fourth of July ferry disgorged visitors who were accompanied by maids, butlers, and nannies. To the relief of most adult natives of the island, the summer residents left on Labor Day as abruptly as they had arrived. But I began to look forward to the beginning of next summer's crossings the day after they had departed.

One particular summer Saturday morning, as I stood among those awaiting passage to the mainland, I watched keenly for someone I'd seen several weeks prior. She was a pretty lady who had caught my attention by waving a white cane extended in front of her--evidence of her blindness. I'd never met a blind person before and was quite intrigued.

Tap, tap, tap. My hopes were rewarded. The lady entered the small cabin of the vintage wooden passenger boat, sat down on the bench opposite me, and opened a large book. Curiosity was killing me. Mom caught me staring and attempted to distract me, but to no avail. My gaze was frozen.

A war waged within my imagination. *She's blind--what's with the book? If she could see me, she might ask me to sit with her.* But there was no way she could be expected to ask me to join her. The next move was up to me. My mother would be aghast. *Should I?*

I shuffled one foot in front of the other, rocked forward off the bench, and catapulted across the deck. Just as I approached her bench, I executed an awkward pirouette and crashed unceremoniously beside her. *There! It was done!*

To my amazement, she spoke first, "I'm so happy to have a young man sit down next to me." *She knew!*

I wanted to know all about her. What happened to her eyes? What was she doing with her fingers?

Her laugh was luscious, hypnotic. The wonderful lady explained that the bumps on the pages were formed into letters called Braille. By sliding her fingers across them she could "see" the letters. Amazing! All too soon, the whistle blew and mom grabbed my hand, muttering what sounded like an apology to the lady. Reluctantly, I parted company with my newfound friend.

I counted the days until I could wheedle my way into making the Saturday crossing again. My patience was rewarded. Tap, tap, tap.

This time I didn't hesitate to take that first step. I ran to her. As if she knew I was coming, she took my hand and we led each other to her seat. "Mickey,"--she had even remembered my name-- "are you able to read?"

"Yes, oh yes!" The letters were typed in bold black beneath the Braille and I began to read to her. You cannot imagine what this did to my heart. I felt so big--so needed. She was special.

My blind friend could have chosen to remain in the safety of her home where the familiarity would simply emphasize her blindness, or she could risk the boat ride. She had chosen to take the risk and in the process rewarded us both.

* * *

For Hal, Joe, and me, who knew so little about the territory into which we were venturing, it was "faith afoot" right from the start. We spent every spare afternoon and weekend charging around Eastern Connecticut following real estate leads and looking at buildings, searching for an available piece of property that might encompass our vision. We were convinced that God was doing something supernatural in and through us. The dreams, influential comments and advice, and the coincidences, drove us along in a "no-turning-back" fashion. Today, I readily regard the dreams as visions, the influential comments as words from the Lord, and the coincidences as divine encounters.

At one point, as we agonized over where the funds for the adventure would come from and how we would secure a property once God revealed it, we experienced something strange, yet distracting. Hal and I were on the phone, wrestling with these very issues, when a third-party voice--male-- interrupted us, saying that he knew of our dilemma and had a solution. My memory is vague, but it had to do with a set of tapes, books, and ultimately some kind of pyramid scheme. The question as to the "source" of this hope threw us both for a loop. We have never figured out how this guy managed to interject himself into our phone conversation, but realize that God preserved us from taking a potentially dangerous, dead-end path.

"This is it! I think we've found it!" The exciting find was on the backside of Gardiner's Lake, in Connecticut. The rambling homestead had no running water, heat, or operating electrical system. It had leaky roofs and smashed windows-- but oh, what potential! We were convinced that God had selected this place and were anxious to tell others. We called a meeting of the neighbors and concerned citizens to share our vision with them.

One of the area residents turned out to be the local sheriff, and he was in attendance. Bullying his way to the front of the group, he announced, that should we go through with the purchase, he would set fire to the building and shoot us as we emerged! (And we wonder where ten and thirteen-year-old gunmen get their ideas!) We had not encountered a particularly cheery group of well wishers. Like curbstones being divined by the cane, this encounter led us elsewhere. Tap, tap, tap. We decided to pass.

Another site Hal and Joe had looked over was a four-story wooden schoolhouse that had served the children of mill workers in Wauregan, Connecticut. The massive structure was much too large and would not suit our needs, but the trip to see it introduced us to the lovely Quinebaug River just down the hill from the property. Joe, two young men, and myself returned several days later to white-water canoe just upstream of the dam.

Two canoes and four inadequately prepared adults pushed off into the icy, turbulent waters just below the Danielson Dam which is located in the town north of Wauregan. Above the next dam, where the two halves of the village of Wauregan are divided by the river, are rapids that challenge even the midsummer enthusiasts. But this was spring. It had only been a week or so since the ice was out and the water was high--and *very* cold.

It must have been the two young'uns 'cause two old veterans like Joe and me wouldn't have floundered in such piece-of-cake rapids! At any rate, one canoe went crossway, the other collided, and together we slammed into an abutment supporting the bridge uniting the villages. Four drenched rats straggled out of the river and up the bank.

Quite providentially, the town tavern was perched at the top of the embankment on our side of the river. "Any port in a storm," as a sharp sailor will quickly quote. Once in the bar, an alcohol-induced neighborliness prevailed. Men ran home and returned with dry clothing. We were fed hot soup and sandwiches. The way these folks responded to our disaster you'd have thought we had stumbled into a church. I've been searching for a church like it ever since!

In the process of introductions, we told them about our burden to set up a home for young men and women who had "crashed and burned." It was in response to the sharing of our vision that one friendly patron suggested the availability of the old schoolhouse up on the hill. Immediately, another friendly drunk suggested that one of the twin mansions built on the hill for the two sons of the original mill owners might be better suited. Of course we had seen them, but we had no idea either of them might be available--or more importantly, affordable. Our curiosity piqued and we made our way up the hill to investigate.

The trek up the hill in borrowed clothes was well worth the effort. What a magnificent Victorian manse! Our sense of elation was soon dampened by the reality that we would never be able to afford such a place. But with God and a vision motivating us, we would not be dissuaded easily. A series of exploratory meetings with the owner, Mrs. Gladys Byles, ensued and she graciously agreed to carry the balance of the loan.

No more bluffing! We were on our way. Only later would we learn the irony of God providing this particular piece of property, which in the 1890s heralded its owner's status above his millworkers, their supervisors, and the church on the hillside below.

When too few take on such a great undertaking it can sabotage a project before it has a fair chance. Our first glimpse of the importance of community would emerge as God providentially sent true servants to partner with us on the hill.

We plunged full steam ahead into a brand new adventure, but what a mess we had charged into! Lots of dirt and work stood between our dream and us. It was daunting but doable. However, for the Moores and Farmers who juggled family and job responsibilities, it was too much. We needed help! God's provision for help became a matter of frequent prayer.

"What are you guys doing in New England?" a regular bookstore customer asked the couple who had been hanging around the shop all morning.

"We don't know, but God led us here," the couple answered.

My antennae was energized. The spiritual wavelength of my newest browsers was foreign to me. For them, "God has something for us in New England," meant selling their meager belongings, packing up their aqua green '62 Chevy BelAir station wagon, and heading east. While camping on relatives' land, they waited to see what God would do. It was during a three-day fast to discover God's leading that they came into the store. Had they heard our prayers?

In disbelief I asked, "Excuse me, I overheard you say you're out here from Michigan. Do I understand correctly that you don't know why you're here?" Within days the decisions were made. The Collins', despite his long hair, her Indian cotton skirt, and their peculiar "leadings," were God's hand-delivered answer to our prayers.

We'd asked God for workers who were able to identify with those we hoped to reach out to. As an aside, we mentioned in our prayers that "it'd be nice" if they had some medical training. Richard and Catherine certainly looked the part and we soon learned that they'd lived the part as well. Drugs and alcohol marked Richard's history prior to his accepting Christ and he'd been a medic in Vietnam. We were shocked! Sometimes the "seed of faith" is so small that I miss it, but it's plenty large enough for God to use.

The nomadic twosome pulled up their tent pegs, but they continued to camp--on the second floor of the mansion. It was August, so room temperature and heat registers went unnoticed. But cold water coming from the hot tap? For Catherine, bathing in a stream had been bearable, but nearly ice-cold water in a nineteenth-century bathtub was different.

Water, boiled in a teakettle over a campstove, was poured into two inches of frigid water in the enamel-over-steel bathtub. She may have thought herself a queen had the steaming water actually raised the temperature!

Richard and Catherine's servanthood proclaimed their allegiance. They loved God and wanted to be used by Him, regardless of personal inconvenience or cost. Their mixture of Pentecostalism and Fundamentalism was foreign to me, but as with most cross-cultural experiences I learned from those I didn't understand.

The whole area of "divine healing," "hearing from God," and "words of knowledge," was new to me. I'd heard of it, but at that time it was lumped together with snake handling, resurrection from the dead, and lengthening of legs! But before me was a couple who talked about this stuff as if they believed that activities which took place when Jesus was on earth were still possible. Not everything was always clear to me, but one thing became very clear--God is God, and He changes not!

Despite the fact that the new couple had a lot to teach us, Joe, Hal, and I decided they were just too young to be at the helm of this program. Joe and Isabelle Wagner joined them along with Wolf, their overly protective German Shepherd. Conservative in their understanding of Christianity, the Wagners added not only balance, but creative tension to the leadership team.

* * *

Zeal? Oh yes, we had plenty of that. Faith? That, too. Vision? More than God allowed us to see at the time. Financial management and business experience? Zip! The need for financial guidance was great and again we prayed for direction from God.

I don't know for sure if the fear I experienced during

these early huge steps of faith was anything akin to that of the blind lady I met on the ferry. I do know that if it hadn't been for those who came alongside me at critical junctures I would have, in all probability, bailed out. Life in the unfamiliar was picking up speed and it was going to be a wild ride.

Again, our unseen Guide was at work. Across the river in nearby Brooklyn, Connecticut lived David Bell, treasurer of a manufacturing firm and a dedicated follower of Christ. When we approached him to serve on our board, Dave didn't see what he could contribute other than the fact that God had blessed him financially. Time has demonstrated that financial resources are the least of his assets.

I needed a friend as much as much as I needed financial advice. Dave became that friend. I have stood before him deserving harsh judgment and have been shown generous grace. By being a part of His Mansion, Dave became a vital link between a community of addicts and misfits and the world of the marketplace.

*   *   *

Along the way we bumped into some proverbial walls and skinned an ankle or two, but now with other hands to guide and help, we'd reached a milestone. A grand old mansion was filled with broken hearts and tormented souls. Young men and women had committed to being used in the process of healing. God's presence was evident and lives were being radically changed, including my own.

When we began this venture I was Sales and Marketing Manager of an international nuclear safety systems manufacturer. I had become accustomed to generous expense accounts, stock options, and credit cards. We lived on the Connecticut shore. We enjoyed dining at the best restaurants on a weekly basis, compliments of the corporation. An unbeatable health insurance plan eliminated a big worry, while a growing port-

insurance plan eliminated a big worry, while a growing port-folio of land around the lakes in New England, investments in American and Canadian coin, vintage automobiles, and coun-try antiques promised to be the basis for our long-term secu-rity.

But as we ventured deeper into the unknown, we left more and more behind. We liquidated coins, cars, land and our antiques were gradually sold off. We drove used beaters donated by sympathetic supporters and friends, sold house-hold furniture in yard sales, and chopped credit cards in half. Beans, hot dogs, and lots of oatmeal, became the staple diet. Restaurant and department store outings became a thing of the past. We accepted gifts of food, clothing, and furniture. At one point, Joan managed the bookstore while I pumped gas at Grandchamp's Texaco and was a Sergeant First Class Drill In-structor in the Army Reserve, one weekend a month. If that were not enough, I also represented a number of publishing companies to the New England Christian booksellers, and con-sulted to the nuclear firm I once worked for.

My wife Joan, is the unsung hero throughout all of this. At the risk of sounding old-fashioned and not yet politically correct, I still maintain that a home--complete with dad, chil-dren, and steady income with benefits--is what most women would choose. Joan gave up all this security and stability when I set out on this journey. There is no such thing as "doing it alone." I don't care what great enterprise you embark upon; others make the trek with you, whether they enlisted or not. It was a painful time for Joan and she felt like her life was being ripped apart. The welfare of her children was at stake. I was totally consumed by the vision and Joan was frightened and often angry. She refused to quit, however, and today every-one who continues in this adventure recognizes who the hero really is. The beginning--the core--of community is spiritual partners who are committed for life. Joan has been that.

*   *   *

58

* * *

We discovered that the *idea* of breaking camp and starting an adventurous journey is usually a lot less stressful than actually *doing* it. The journey will be far more fulfilling if one takes the time to count the cost in advance. There'll be strugglers (and stragglers) along the way who neglected to plan ahead and consequently, are so hopelessly swamped that they have little or no hope of ever reaching their goal. Be kind and gentle with them; they need it. You'll appreciate it when the roles are reversed. Those of us further along the path must be careful to remember from whence we came!

The world that once had been so familiar now seemed strangely distant. We were committed to follow the path before us. There would be no turning back.

"Donuts." I never knew his real name. He had one I'm sure, but on an island a nickname is all you need. He was our island safety officer--a combination of police chief, fire chief, and Truant Officer.

Donuts could be found every afternoon faithfully standing at his post in the "firebarn," a two-unit garage with a small outhouse attached. The firebarn--housing one red truck, shiny nozzles, axes, and a row of special hats--held a magical fascination for most boys. Along the wall, in the corner of the firehouse, there was a huge brass bell and a ticker-tape running through a maze of switches. Once a fire alarm was initiated, the bell rang and the ticker tape directed coded strings of whistles heard island-wide, summoning volunteers.

Donuts had a couple of bad habits that were well known by most of the lads on the island. One, was the flask he kept hidden in his jacket from which he drew courage to face the impending daily threats; the other, his private stash of "girlie" magazines kept hidden in the outhouse. Each afternoon, Donuts retired to his "study" to read, often becoming weary in well doing and leaning his head against the door for a snooze. From time-to-time my schoolmates had gone into the firebarn and awakened Donuts from his bathroom reverie, so his patterns were well known.

The idea for my latest prank initially formed as bored stiff, I stared into space daydreaming about life outside of the brick walls. It is true that the adventures promising the most potential are also fraught with greater risk. In my experience, the anticipation of mischief and laughter is nearly as entertaining as the actual event. Imagining an escapade and visualizing the possible outcome is fifty percent of the finished product--but only when I've decided to go through with it *regardless* of the risks.

On the way home I peeked through the open overhead door. I could hear Donuts' soft, steady snore emanating from the outhouse. Grasping the knurled two-foot stick I'd selected for the task, I tiptoed into the barn and rapped the big brass alarm bell for all I was worth. Next on my agenda was to join Roger Bannister and those fleet-footed track stars who followed him, in running a four-minute mile!

My last glimpse of the inside of the firebarn was the outhouse door flying open and Donuts toppling out on his knees--his pants down around his ankles!

The Peaks Island Telephone Company--consisting of "the operator," a board full of holes and a bundle of cords each with a prong on the end--was headquartered adjacent to the firehouse. Mary Groggins, telephone operator and island gossip, spied me running faster than usual just as the alarm went off. One cord hung from the headset Mary wore harnessed about her neck and the other pronged end shot straight for the hole on the board connected to the Farmers. With one hand operating the prong, the other was busy turning the black crank; ringers sang out in six homes. A series of rings signaled our home, but you can be sure that five additional ladies pressed receivers to their ears. Before I made it home the entire island knew who the culprit was! What had started out as my own personal escapade ended up being exposed for the entire island community to gossip about.

*   *   *

We would all prefer a smooth road to our destination but seldom is this the way life works out--especially when human nature is added to the mix! This was certainly true for the fledgling work known as His Mansion. Potholes will appear unexpectedly out of nowhere, while the biggest hazards we seem to fashion ourselves.

This was certainly true the weekend several His Mansion students struck out for a weekend Bible conference at Word of Life Bible Institute at Schroon Lake. A little suds, song, and occasional lovemaking became the substitute agenda. The "messages" must have been inspiring because whereas four people left on Friday, five returned Sunday night. This fifth, invisible member, remained a "stowaway" for several months.

It was shortly after this incident that I was dubbed "Director" of His Mansion Ministries. This was frightening, as I was a novice at dealing with the responsibilities I had assumed. Maureen, who'd been living at His Mansion for some time, remained in the office to help me over some of the hurdles. She was a great asset and in addition to serving as my administrative assistant, she served as a room counselor.

One day I discovered Maureen crying in the office. "Stan, I'm pregnant," she announced. The mysterious stowaway had been discovered. She had been party to the infamous Schroon Lake scandal. Ironically, Maureen actually attended another conference at Word of Life just two weeks after the reckless weekend, but was as yet, unaware of the small human heart beating inside her. In the course of this second exposure to the message of God's Word, the Holy Spirit gave new life to her wounded heart and prompted grief over her sin. In the months that followed, although she experienced a spiritual renewal, she fully expected to be asked to leave when she exposed her now known condition. Despite her fears, Maureen confessed and with the confession also came forgiveness.

My mind didn't have time to think about the implications before I blurted out, "Praise the Lord!"

"Praise the Lord?" she was confused. "Praise the Lord?" It was a beauty for ashes thing. I replied:

"Yes, I am praising the Lord because you chose life when other alternatives are so readily available and would have erased the immediate problem." To me this was confirmation that the course we had plotted was a worthy one. That's what this adventure is about--bringing forth new life from ashes.

64

*   *   *

In my enthusiasm for nurturing new life through the ministry under my direction, I lost sight of a mother and two children--*my* own wife and two children!

The process was killing Joan. Unable to pay our bills, we began selling off our antiques and furnishings. The loss of medical insurance was traumatic but the biggest loss to my family, which I failed to comprehend at the time, was the absence of a husband and father. A vacuum was building in their lives. How could I have been so blind?

One morning, when I was leaving home to go to the Mansion, I announced to Joan my intention to take her vacuum cleaner along because the workcrew ladies needed it to clean the huge house. It sounds simple, doesn't it? But the new appliance was my gift to Joan on her recent birthday. It was a bottom-of-the-line Sears model because that was all we were able to afford. A year before, I'd have had someone install a central vacuum cleaning system in our house, regardless of cost, but our circumstances had changed.

"No, you cannot take the vacuum with you," Joan protested. "*That place* already has everything I own. You've even sold the kitchen table and chairs!" Joan made her impassioned plea, but I prevailed. We agreed that I could take the vacuum, but should I arrive home without it--or any piece of it--I could find someplace else to spend the night!

It also happened to have been one of those Fridays when teachers take a day off with pay and label it "teacher's conferences." We all know better! The children were home, so I offered to take Shawn and Sherree with me, which softened Joan some.

I arrived at the Mansion and handed over the vacuum cleaner with strict orders that they must, *must*, send it back with me--every piece--when I left for the day. They used it all day and were extremely careful to see that it was returned with every piece intact. I'd have a place to sleep that night.

Upon arriving home, I threw open the door, and in a sarcastic tone announced, "Here's your lousy vacuum cleaner!"

Joan looked down at the pile, then at me in disbelief. She began to cry, out of anger, not hurt. "Stan Farmer, where are my children?" I had remembered the vacuum cleaner but had forgotten Shawn and Sherree!

Not long after this incident, I assigned Joan a responsibility for which she felt she required further direction. "I've got a question for you, Stan," she said. "Not now, Joan, I don't have time right now," I impatiently replied.

She could take no more. The voice in her head began to scream, *I can't stand it any longer. I hate this place!* All I heard was the door slam and the sound of her feet running down the driveway.

I stopped everything and made the mistake of following her. A mile or so down the road, I spotted her small frame pumping its way away from me. Pulling up beside her I asked Joan to get into the car and talk to me, but she yelled, "No!" When it looked as if I would persist, Joan pointed to an elderly man who stood watching us from his yard. "If you continue to harass me, I'm gonna scream my head off. He'll call the police. Leave me alone!" Years later, Joan revealed that she just "needed some space!"

Joan had come to a life-changing decision that day. She stopped trying to fit in where she felt she was unwanted but at the same time was expected to display all the attributes of sainthood. She didn't need to please me, or to please His Mansion. She needed only to please God. God had called her to be a mom and that was the path she would follow.

Not long afterward, Joan took her first paying job since

we were married--at a nearby convalescent home. Once our children left for school for the day, she reported for work. Preparing meals for the elderly provided Joan with something I had failed to provide. She was talented, needed, wanted, and appreciated.

* * *

Through stressful occasions like this, and unexpected situations within the ministry, I learned to expect many types of frustration. It would require wisdom to see the warning signs and to avoid the bumps in the road. The key would be in exercising the wisdom to attend to the most important relationships first and not get distracted. Every day seemed to stretch our limited experience and distract my focus. An incident involving a student named Amy illustrates this vividly.

Amy's torment of rolling around on the floor, falling into furniture, moaning and groaning had kept others in the dorm up for three nights straight. Her episode began around midnight each evening. Interns prayed, read the Bible out loud, and tried to keep her from hurting herself.

Despite their effort, Amy continued to be tormented. Furthermore, the "manifestations" multiplied whenever Scripture was read. This troubled her mentors. *God is more powerful...Isn't He?* they wondered. Not only that, they yearned for a good night's sleep!

Amy was moved into the quarters where her mentors slept. They had to be up with her anyway, so why keep everyone else awake? As the specter of a fourth night loomed, the team gathered to pray. Tom and Jim, two directors, received Amy's permission to station themselves outside of her door. Two more team members committed themselves to pray at a place removed from the action.

Midnight approached and Tom and Jim met in Tom's office. They would rather be home with their families but had sensed that this was not your average behavioral struggle.

This was warfare of a far different stripe. As they waited, Tom prayerfully wondered what he had gotten himself--and everyone else--into! The answer was simply, "It's your job!" As if cueing him to punch in, the call came. It was midnight.

Three women were already in the second-floor room with Amy when Jim and Tom arrived. While Joy and Deb chased Amy around the room with pillows to keep her from hurting herself, the men sat in the hallway across from the open doorway. They joined in the prayer and Bible reading while keeping a close eye on Amy. Each time Scripture was spoken, Amy became more agitated.

While watching the action, Tom felt a growing suspicion. A veteran of employment in correctional facilities, he had seen far more serious attempts at self-destruction. Meanwhile, Jim--a skeptic by nature--consciously tried to give her the benefit of the doubt. Tom had seen enough and beckoned Jim to retreat so they could caucus. As they met in the stairwell, Tom admitted, "I'm trying to be as compassionate as possible, but this is really bothering me."

Jim concurred, "I can't shake the feeling that we're being 'had'."

"I wish I had something that sounded like Scripture but wasn't." Jim's eyes lit up. He'd been thinking the same thing.

"Like the *Qur'ān*?" he asked, imagining the King James sound-alike as a litmus test.

"Yeah, you got one?"

"Over in my office." "Well, go get it!"

Jim returned with the book and began to read, "And verily the Lord is He, the Exalted in Might, Most Merciful." Predictably the commotion increased. When Amy settled down, he began to read once more, "So call not on any other god with God." Amy moaned all the louder. "Or thou wilt be among those under the Penalty."

When the reading had stopped, the eerie groaning subsided and Jim did all he could to keep from laughing aloud!

Pulling himself together, he proceeded to read again: "Proclaim! In the name of thy Lord and Cherisher who created--created man, out of a clot of congealed blood." Amy moaned even louder. Huh? After hearing the unfamiliar "scripture," the staff women looked at Jim with suspicion. Jim and Tom exchanged knowing glances.

Jim entered the room and said, "You know, Amy, I don't know what's going on, but I get the same kind of reaction whether I read the Bible or whether I read the Qur'ān." In short, he said, "I don't buy it!"

"I knew they wouldn't believe me," Amy mumbled under her breath as she sat up. Amy had tried her best to pull off the old "the devil made me do it" routine but had gotten caught. The sleep-deprived women who had prayed and consoled the resident Oscar winner felt violated--but also relieved. God's Word always triumphs over evil, but in this case it was just another case of a rebellious, attention-starved, human heart!

More than one person benefited from this ordeal. Amy deserved to be dismissed but was offered compassion instead. Tom's faith continues to be strengthened, as he remembers God's presence with them as they met on the stairwell outside of the room.

Jim verbalized the question that begged to be asked. "Was Amy really demon possessed?" No. But could there be demonic influence? A resounding yes! The mysterious, yet powerful component of the human makeup that is known as "soul," is the target of dark forces who seek to twist and ruin all that is good in the human potential was surely at work. The entire drama was far beyond anything one would call normal or easily explainable.

Normal or not, the lesson remains. It is not a matter of our personal knowledge or experience as much as it is being confident that God is all-powerful, and present on our journey, no matter how twisted the path may become.

*   *   *

This truth was certainly applicable the day we lost Jan. She was a troubled girl who was very frightened. She reminded me of a puppy that was convinced she would be beaten every time someone in authority approached. Jan would cower and draw away, a washed-out, straggly wisp. One morning Isabelle found the note, "I am too hurt. No one cares. I can't go on. I'm sorry." It was signed, "Jan."

Panic ensued. We searched high and low and interviewed all the residents, to no avail. I remember my heart being tight with fear anticipating what I might encounter when I removed the cover from an old well in the field. Years later, I can still feel the foreboding that I felt that night as I ventured down into the dark catacomb-like basement so typical of large Victorian manses. I just knew I'd round the corner to bump into a hanging body!

Several days passed. Additional notes indicating the intention to commit suicide, were discovered. They had been strategically placed between stacked towels in the laundry. There was still no sight of Jan. Relatives had heard nothing and it was looking bad. I feared that in the end the stench of decaying flesh would lead us to the terrible, inevitable truth.

Over the course of subsequent days, Isabelle noticed that food was missing and without telling anyone else, she formulated a plan. One evening, after "lights out," Isabelle powdered the rear staircase, once used by the mansion's servants, with talcum powder and set her alarm for very early morning. Sure enough, there were the tiny footprints leading down and up the steps to the second floor, the third floor, into the attic, and right up to the wall! Upon close inspection, we found a small bowtie latch that allowed the matchboard panel to be removed, providing access to a large crawl space under the eaves. There we found a cooking pot being used for toilet, a bottle of water, box of crackers, pillow--and Jan. She was quite alive!

A week later we found another set of notes written by Jan. As before, we could not find her. A month later she surfaced in New Haven, alive and well! Jan has since married and raised a family.

* * *

We have experienced many such deceptive dramas along the way and over time they tend to produce a spirit of cynicism. Looking for the humor and laughing when you can, holds the secret to being able to offer the next person the benefit of the doubt. There have been many opportunities to laugh--and cry!

During the early years of the ministry, I conducted Bible studies for a handful of zealous young men. These guys lived in the Norwich area and several of them roomed together. At this particular time, the hot topic among the "Jesus People" was demon possession and how to purge oneself--and others--from the critters! "OUT IN THE NAME OF JESUS!!" could be heard at almost any gathering of intense young believers. Unfortunately, it is one of those tasty soundbytes that become callously misused.

A phone call came late one afternoon from a supermarket manager in Norwich. "I've got a couple of young men in here who have been disruptive, and they claim you are their teacher and that what they have been doing is what you have taught them." I was immediately off to Norwich to rescue the religious fanatics!

They had gone shopping together for their weekly grocery supplies and the trouble started when they came across a snack item labeled, "Devil Dogs." One of the guys started shouting, "Out in the name of Jesus," at the top of his lungs. (Whether these misguided zealots were serious or joking in poor taste, never became clear to me.)

71

This passed without too much notice until Frank came to the aisle where he spotted "Underwood Deviled Ham." The cry went up again this time attracting the attention of elderly shoppers who were frightened out of their skins! This display put the manager over the edge and he invited the rabid threesome outside for a little chat. Great evangelism opportunity!

A year later several young men who had served together in the program moved into an apartment in nearby Wauregan. Bad feelings had broken out among the "brothers," and they concluded that evil spirits were at fault--another twist on the "devil-made-me-do-it" theme. Remembering the New Testament story about Jesus casting the demons into pigs and sending them into the drink, the guys came up with a solution. One of them had a pet guinea pig...you're catching on, aren't you? Down to the bridge over the Quinebaug river--hocus, pocus and glug, glug, glug. The pig was in the river and back in the apartment iron continued to sharpen iron! The need for more Bible instruction while going through His Mansion's program became all too clear.

*　　*　　*

Work projects frequently produced an ample supply of laughter and frustration. "Michael the Archangel" was a major contributor. His name was really Michael, but I don't know for sure where the rest of his moniker came from. This young veteran of the counterculture was severely "tapped out" from acid use. Drug induced schizophrenia had set in hard and Michael had regular communication with entities in the Vapor, hence the "angel," I suppose.

My experience and interaction with hippie "roadwarriors" during my salesman days had provided valuable insight concerning what might be going on in twisted minds and gave me the incentive to persevere with Michael.

"Trippers" would often describe in detail a variety of "beings" encountered while under the influence of LSD. It is my theory that these mind-bending chemicals are the potions used by the "Charming One--the Great Enchanter," referred to in the Greek Testaments (Septuagint) and the New Testaments as "Pharmekia." Interestingly enough, this is also the Greek word from which our English word, *pharmacy*, is derived. The "old drug store!"

The friendly, humanlike animal characters of '50s Disneyland evolved into frightening other-worldly creatures in the cartoons of the '60s and '70s. The young adults tripping on LSD were having up-close-and-personal encounters with the actual characters during their acid-induced excursions into other dimensions. I was treated to many vivid descriptions from recovering druggies.

Man has been instructed and warned over and over again in Scripture not to delve into the area of "unseen things," the spirit world, the world of other dimensions. This is referred to as witchcraft, sorcery, and necromancy in the Old Testament. It is for our welfare and safety that God placed a delicate barrier in our consciousness. Mind-altering drugs and "transcendental exercises" can pierce that fragile barrier, permitting entry beyond the veil. Thousands of otherwise bright young men and women, each with great potential, visited that other world, only to be tormented by memories--flashbacks--for the remainder of their lives. Michael the Archangel was but one of a growing army of fractured "space travelers" taking up residence in parks, rest homes, alleys, curbsides, and rehab programs.

It was difficult finding work for Michael, because although he was here in body, his mind spent most of the time on Planet Zoar. Bob Whitehead, the work supervisor, decided that Michael could push a lawnmower without too much difficulty. It seemed to be a good decision as Michael zoomed around the campus lawns for several hours.

Just before lunch, Whitehead went out to check on Michael's progress. I could hear Bob roar from my second-floor office perch at the rear of the building. Michael had run the mower over the entire estate, but the grass was just as high as when he began! Upon close inspection, it was discovered that he had reset the wheel height so that the mower cut just above the grass tips. Michael claimed that when he started cutting he could hear the grass screaming in excruciating pain and that he couldn't stand to inflict such torture on other "living things." So much for creative work assignments!

Of course, humor can be dangerously close to disaster, as happened when a state caseworker arrived to visit Al. The young man was one of those troubled sixteen-year-olds caught in the bureaucratic black hole that exists in the gap between child and adult services. Al was angry, frightened, and very small in stature for his age--almost diminutive. This would not be his first placement as none before had been acceptable to him nor had host families accepted him. Nothing in Al's countenance signaled hope for this arrangement.

But at His Mansion, Al finally found a place where he felt wanted and loved. In the weeks to follow, we witnessed a transformation in both his countenance and vocabulary. His willing, upbeat attitude became an encouragement to everyone.

Behind the grand manse, a huge stone-lined cistern received all the sewage and waste flowing from the main building and the servants' quarters. One day, the cesspool overflowed. It had clogged up, preventing the liquid from escaping to the leach fields. A basic physics lesson was in the making. Water takes the path of least resistance. Raw sewage began to fill the basement of the Carriage House. I was just about to call the local septic man when 'Little Al' grabbed a shovel and started digging. I had reservations about this, knowing that his social worker was due to pay a visit later in the day. It would be great if he was at least clean. But no such luck!

74

Al dropped the shovel and it disappeared from sight in the gross soup of sewage that bore eerie resemblance to a primordial tar pit. Before anyone could stop him, Al, a prototype Indiana Jones, tied a rope around a tree and his waist and slipped into the cesspool--just as the State of Connecticut compact rolled up the driveway.

"Look out, it's one of those buggies with the State Seal on the door." The warning came from an alert secretary. It was Al's caseworker who had come to check up on her charge. As soon as she spotted me across the lawn, the caseworker shouted, "Where's Al?"

Before I could run interference, one of the more gregarious students volunteered, "Oh, he's the guy tied to the tree over there." So much for making a good impression! The social worker--the product of a large inner-city family herself--quickly picked up on the comedy of errors and joined us in a hearty laugh.

* * *

In addition to humor and laughter, thanksgiving for God's power and our appreciation for the people that He brings into our lives can help smooth the ride. After Maureen had shared with me her secret that she was pregnant, she was understandably shaken. It was imperative that I am home for supper, but I dreaded leaving with Maureen upset, so I was relieved to meet our newest staff member coming in the door as I was heading out. Rick Madden was just the man for the job. As we passed in the doorway, I handed him a choice assignment. "Maureen just found out that she's pregnant; please take care of her."

Rick was a Medical Corpsman stationed in Groton, Connecticut, with the U. S. Navy. He had found his way into the Bread of Life Bookstore and into our hearts. The vision of His Mansion was contagious and Rick caught it. He committed himself to serve evenings and weekends at the facility. A month later the Navy actually assigned Rick, as a part of Project Transition, to serve at His Mansion for the remainder of his enlistment!

Maureen had her baby while she was a resident of His Mansion. As her pregnancy became more and more obvious, the sense of anticipation grew in all of us. It was as if God was giving us a gift. During the months of her pregnancy, Rick had grown to love Maureen and the life within her. Rick had been sent away on business when the time came for Maureen to have her baby, so I took his place pacing the hospital floor. "It's a boy!" Rick and Maureen were married later that year and began life together with little Brian in tow. Looking back to the day of his arrival and my instruction that he look after Maureen, Rick laughs, "You never told me when to stop."

Rick was our resident everything! Assistant director, room discipler, outreach coordinator--you name it, he did it. The rudimentary classes in Bible application became the solid underpinning of Rick's faith, but not all those vital lessons were learned in the classroom. Some of them were demonstrated in God's daily provision for us.

Although the mortgage payment always went out on time, money was tight. We'd get behind with the power company and they'd threaten to shut off the power. The phones were in jeopardy too. And people needed to eat. These needs were always met.

* * *

Joan and I had watched our savings and investments dwindle as God gave us the privilege of "not letting the right hand know what the left hand was doing." The bills were in fact, being paid and the bottom of our personal financial security barrel was now shiny. The Moores had sacrificed all that they could and all of the Farmers' resources were gone. It was as if we had passed a test. Yet the hardships we endured were rewarded as we saw God's provision. Once, while praying around a dinner table that displayed a lot of wood and very little food, a bread truck driven by someone we'd never met offered the hungry household all of his day-old stock. On another day, a bag of groceries mysteriously appeared on the kitchen counter. The His Mansion family literally lived off of what the Lord provided, resulting in more than one exciting Epicurean adventure! A student once prayed before supper, "Dear Lord, please make this edible. Amen."

One time a commercial fisherman from Connecticut was the vehicle God used. His son had been in our program. The man showed up with a 55-gallon drum filled with fresh flounder. Filet of Sole! What a gourmet delight, unless you had to skin and clean them.

The barrel was carried to the basement and three of us began cleaning them after supper. At midnight we were still cleaning fish--I was the only original worker still at it. The others had succumbed to nausea and vomiting as the halfway point in the barrel was reached. Our arms sunk deep into slimy fish-fluids, and the smell was enough to cause one to consider the merits of starvation. Sometime after midnight and six inches from the bottom of the barrel, my stomach revolted. But for weeks the family enjoyed the delight of fried filet of flounder.

There was a time when food was so scarce that anything left over from breakfast--pancake pieces, French toast crumbs, scrapings from the oatmeal pots--ended up in the soup-of-the-day at lunch. After a month of this, it was getting old for some of the volunteers. One day at lunch, the server lifted the lid off a large pot, lowered the ladle, and came up with one of Sam's sneakers. It was a joke, of course, but too close to home! What does Michael Jordan say? "Just do it?" No way!

77

And if it wasn't shoes, it was mystery meat. Driving home one day, I spotted a snapper turtle crossing the highway. That night no one was very interested in the evening entree of turtle soup, but a day later when we had "beef stew" everyone was delighted! Chicken chow mein made with wingless, four-legged chicken drew raves until it was deduced that it was really squirrel shot out back by my son, Shawn. Although I struggled with the deceptive nature of the ploys, the need to encourage the family to consume needed protein overcame it. Meat is meat, after all!

Our faith was certainly bolstered by these dramatic demonstrations of God's provision, but carelessness and foolhardiness were mixed with that faith. We were on a God-ordained journey, not one for which we were necessarily prepared in advance. As Rick says, "God was using me in people's lives and there was no reason why He should. I had no training. I did some really stupid things. But God used them anyway. God protected us while we were a young and stupid ministry."

On the mornings the mortgage payments were due, Rick remembers walking down the hill to the post office, knowing that the checkbook never held enough to meet the $365 bill. But P. O. Box 256 always held the difference. "Every time--often right on that day--the money would come," Rick explains.

For those who travel such journeys, these are more than fond memories--they're memorials. Rick explains, "It's almost like when the Israelites crossed the Jordan River and set up the stones of remembrance. Often I look back when I'm going through times of testing or situations where I need faith. Looking at some of those experiences gives me confidence that God is faithful and He's gonna come through. It might be at the last minute, but I don't really need to worry."

*   *   *

A major mistake, and one often made, is to focus all of our attention on the potholes in the road only to miss the beauty that surrounds us. Early in the last century it was a common practice for small communities to sponsor several local parades throughout the year. There were opportunities to feature the best of the years harvest, the strongest or fastest animals—and occasionally, exceptional people. It was called "parading out your best."

A community's civic pride in having offered their sons and daughters to insure this country's freedom would be demonstrated in parades as veterans of our wars represented their units and community.

I need to be reminded from time-to-time, of the winners, achievers, and heroes that are a part of my journey. Live is not one long flat expanse of terrain pockmarked by potholes, even though it may appear that way at times.

Our second child, Sherree, was the product of the same environment and influences as our son Shawn. Same mom, same dad, same deal. Sherree listened to the same arguments and watched the same tears flow. She witnessed the identical acts of compassion, and rejoiced over the same answered prayers.

Throughout her childhood years Sherree provided nothing but joy and pleasure. Public schools were in decline in the 80's and Sherree was then in high school. Almost as soon as she entered high school, Sherree began to emerge as a leader. Throughout her four years, her peers drafted her for class officer or the head of this-or-that committee. She lettered in four sports and was clearly one of the most popular students—among men and women!

A Sherree's graduation the principal who chaired the event asked that the audience hold their applause until all recipients had received their diplomas—with the exception of the Valedictorian and salutatorian. The diplomas were issued one after the other in alphabetical order without interruption, until the letter "F" approached. Here Mr. Norton stopped the process and made comment: "I must now make an exception to my own edict. The following student is an exception and has been a blessing to this school every time she has crossed the threshold." At that point the audience burst into unanimous applause. Sherree was that exception.

Hillsboro High was in the semi-finals for the woman's state championship that year. It was the last half with sixteen seconds left in the game. Hillsboro was down by one point and a Hillsboro player put the ball in play at the half court line. Sherree took the ball in play and to the heart-stopping amazement of her coach didn't pass the ball in toward the basket, but pivoted, set her feet, and shot from just a few feet inside the half court line. Time was frozen as the ball made a long curved arc, coming down straight through the cord. Hillsboro was the winner. Sherree was a winner.

The culture we live in, encourages us to either hide our mistakes and mask our flaws, or to expose *only* the worst about ourselves or others, when we do open up. This is not healthy and gives rise to discouragement at best, and deceptiveness at worse. Parades are fast becoming a thing of the past. We need to revive the concept.

* * *

The Sherrees—and they exist—are rare. The tendency is to not consider the highest and lowest scores and average everything else. Wrong! Keep your eye out for the exceptions. Celebrate them. Walk along side of them when you get the chance. Learn from them. Ask them: "What?— Why?—and "How." But do not overlook a much more readily available source of encouragement as we struggle through life, and that is the occasional—perhaps unexpected— victories and high achievements by those ordinary folks who are making the trip along with us.

Don't wait to see if today's exception will continue to pull it off day after day, before you celebrate and affirm. Give credit to the valiant efforts of today. Affirm your fellow sojourner when he or she does the momentary, or incidental laudable act. So what if tomorrow their star doesn't shine. There is a far greater chance that a glow will still be evident tomorrow if we stop and polish it up today. Life is too short to keep long accounts and unreasonable standards for holding a parade.

VI. DISASTERS AND DEADENDS!

Whenever we are engaged in a life-changing, no-turning-back venture, a sinister fear hovers in our consciousness that some catastrophic incident might ruin the dream. But don't cancel the trip because of what might happen. Disasters may come frighteningly close. The cost of pursuing the dream may exact a far greater price than we dare to imagine. But if our destination is really worth pursuing, we'll take the risks and press on despite the obstacles ahead.

My dad served aboard a flat-bottomed gunboat on the Yangtze River during the '30s when the Japanese invasion of China was about to start. In that peculiar, isolated duty station unorthodox practices were not uncommon, including the keeping of a ship's mascot, which in this case was a mischievous mongrel. My father had caught the cur in the galley and gave it a helping hand out through the entryway--more accurately a boot--while shouting after it, "you lousy bum!" The "Coolie" cook quickly came to the mutt's defense with an expletive that amounted to "Mitty-bum," which roughly translated means, "No bum!" When the ship returned to the United States, the dog was still aboard. Somewhere along the five-thousand mile passage home, my tough-fisted dad, veteran of a dozen boiler room boxing venues, had fallen in love with the useless mutt.

The original Mitty-Bum met his end long before my dad left the service. Soon after beginning a family, however, dad brought home a near duplicate white Spitz Terrier, with its characteristic black eye and matching dark ear, and perfectly shaped black mustache over his hind end.

Few human beings have ever held a place deeper in my heart than Mitty-Bum. We were inseparable. By my early teens we'd moved from my isolated island to the mainland. A new challenge in my new environment was crossing Route 25, which divided our farm from our neighbor's. This was the first highway with which I'd ever dealt.

I trained Mitty-Bum to sit on the shoulder until I crossed the highway, then come when I whistled. Upon hearing the signal he'd eagerly bound across without a sideways glance-- trusting me completely. The day came when I needed to go across, but didn't want the dog to accompany me. Faithful friend that he was, he waited until I was just out of sight then sneaked along after me. When I was halfway up the neighbor's driveway, Mitty-Bum made his fateful sprint across the highway to join me. The trucker never saw the white and black blur, and roared away, totally unaware. His body broken, Mitty-Bum died instantly. My heart was broken. Tears can still sneak out if I let my guard down and relive the incident.

Today I realize this traumatic lesson of life, love, and loss could hardly have been learned in a less costly way. Life is a delicate balance of life and death, love and loss. I'm reminded that the greatest love and joy I've experienced in my life came at the expense of the death of God's only Son! That delicate balance has played itself out in my own journey and in the journey of His Mansion.

* * *

The Schroon Lake Scandal, combined with several other near-disasters, convinced me that the practice of leaving young, inexperienced staff to guard the fort was out of the question. Even though it meant leaving my family alone forty miles away, I felt that I had to be there.

I was on a mission and it had to succeed, and I believed that I was the one to make it happen. It was a bad call. I would not recommend this line of reasoning to couples starting out on their life-journey today. The process wounded my family--wounds that have healed but from which the scars are still visible.

I spent four days and three nights at the Mansion, three days and four nights home and also operated a retail business that was an outreach to the community but which produced no income for us. Joan was getting the short end of the stick. Not only was she being ripped away from a safe, supportive community but I also had little emotional energy left for her.

In the midst of this chaos, stress, and tension there was a light at the end of the tunnel, but it was not the light of day. It was the beacon of an impending moral disaster. It approached like an oncoming freight train and I should have seen it coming. I didn't. Blinded by exhaustion, pride, and self - pity, I was still grinning when it hit me.

I couldn't blame the breakdown on lack of experience in extremely stressful situations as I was familiar with them. Once, while on board the submarine USS BARBEL (SS 580), during an enemy attack in the Bay of Tonkin, we plummeted into the darkness of the Pacific and came to rest more than a hundred feet below test depth. As the powerful hands of the deep tried to squeeze the air out of us, the hull began to compress. Signs of immanent destruction were abundant: Pipes wrenched, metal creaked and groaned, a gasket in a small seawater line burst. The non-ductile enamel paint, which coats the inside of the hull, began to splinter, chip, and fill the air. At any minute I expected we'd all be squeezed into a space the size of a basketball.

In the midst of the crisis a shipmate, nicknamed "The Deacon" because of his atheistic, blasphemous tirades, blurted out, "God ain't got the @#! to crush this submarine!" I grabbed a 15-inch Crescent wrench and went after him. "I'm going to kill you, before He kills us all just to shut you up," I shouted. My fellow throttleman, "Ski," intervened and may have saved the Deacon's life! But this crisis was far different!

*   *   *

I'm sure I was not aware of the insidious advancement of sick thinking as it worked its way into my psyche, but that it found a welcome home, cannot be questioned. People needed me. I solved problems. God was doing miracles, no doubt. But I began to believe I was responsible for whether the mission failed or succeeded.

The term coined for this phenomenon is "Messiah Complex," and it is an apt description. The staff sought me out; they needed me. The phone rang all hours of the night. I felt it was my responsibility to rescue heroin addicts from "shooting galleries" where a person could be shot or stabbed to death for no other reason than for being there. I felt I needed to stay up all night wrestling with someone who was under the control of dark, evil forces. In ignorance, arrogance, and pride, I opened myself up to the same destructive influences against which I fought. In the midst of this mind bending chaos I was, piece by piece, constructing the very locomotive that would eventually run me over. The fear of being compressed into a sphere of flesh aboard the submarine paled in comparison to the fear, confusion, and despair I felt as the freight roared off into the distance having flattened me and left those close to me in shambles.

Joan had sacrificed a life of financial security for herself and the children. She gave up the opportunity for social involvement with real people--normal people. The Mansion became the mistress I had chosen over her. This assessment being painfully accurate, it is safe to say our relationship was under great strain and certainly not healthy!

Where an appetite exists, there's an instinct to satisfy it. Opportunities for self-exaltation and self-satisfaction are always knocking and the ear attuned will surely hear them. I began to listen for the sounds that would satisfy my bloated ego. While reaching out to rescue others, I became mired in my own quicksand. Being the only one who could rescue, I had left no one in position to rescue me. There were a few people who knew I was sinking, but because of my own ability to deceive, and their respect for me, I was left to choke on my own vomit.

When Jim Jones did his awful thing at Jonestown, people were baffled at how a man, who was once a minister in good standing in a major denomination, could end up an egotistical, suicidal maniac. I have no problem understanding it. It isn't difficult. Anyone can do it! Take on more than you can handle. Don't eat properly. Add a big dose of sleep deprivation. Operate in a theater where little or no accountability exists. Subject yourself to a constant barrage of the worst sexual, sensual, and morbid testimonies imaginable. Now try unraveling this mayhem in your own strength. If good things happen, the apparent results convince your ego that you are responsible. You'll feel like the Pied Piper, but you can't see your own path. You'll end up crashing into some horrible ravine. If you're fortunate--that is, forced to see yourself and your path for what it is and repent--you may get to live again. If not, you drink the Kool-Aid along with all those you have misled.

I began to convince myself that everything was going wonderful, people were being healed, and I was the guru responsible for it all. This sick, skewed perception of oneself is where cult leaders are born. Fortunately, this up-and-coming Jim Jones was killed by a freight train of his own making. Psychologists and psychiatrists have elaborate names for this set of circumstances: stress syndrome, chronic fatigue, etc. But the Great Physician's diagnosis needs no second opinion: It is sin.

In the course of this dismal parenthesis in my life, I made some particularly sinful choices that in turn produced painful consequences. However, in the midst of the turmoil, chaos, and sin, a correct choice--a right choice--was also made. Just as poor choices produce negative natural consequences, right choices produce positive consequences. In this case honoring the sanctity of life over convenience, resulted in a very special daughter named Erin. She is now twenty-six, married, the mother of two wonderful children, and a follower of Jesus.

The magnitude of my sin shocked me back into reality. Broken and contrite, God, in His mercy, provided me with a guide in the form of an aged, wise, compassionate pastor who was also a skilled counselor. He recognized my need for accountability, for both my own well being and the ministry's. His advice took root, and I began to realize the need to bring in additional long-term staff to help shoulder the burden. I recognized my need to delegate and take my hands off of

I recognized my need to delegate and take my hands off of matters that I really had no experience or gift to handle. Immediately, I gave others more responsibility for what we referred to as "counseling." The truth is, I have little gift for counseling. I don't have a great capacity for absorbing someone else's pain and helping them with it.

God's Word is powerful and sharp. It is effective because it is true, even when the messenger is off the wall! Through the faithfulness of young men and women whose motives were pure and whose minds were stable, many were helped and delivered from mental and emotional bondage--despite the disturbed state of my own mind. But others were negatively affected. Several were hurt. Many were disappointed. But none were overlooked or forsaken by God.

Out of the ashes of my moral failure came someone who is far less sure of himself; who is desperately in need of others to carry on the work; and who is acutely aware of the One who is the Author of every good thing!

I have been broken, but not busted. I am guilty, but not condemned. I am limited, but not useless. I know a God of mercy and of grace!

* * *

My personal crisis of character wasn't the only event threatening the work God was building: One morning, from the picture window in my living room, I spotted dark plumes of smoke in the sky. As I speculated on the source, the ringing of the telephone jolted me. It was Dave Hultgren announcing that His Mansion was on fire!

My mind involuntarily flashed back to the day when the estate next to ours--a twin mansion built as a gift for the twin brother to the original owner of ours, burst into flames. They had been built so close together that everyone in our building had to be evacuated. Local firefighters predicted that would go up in the intense heat. Walnut, mahogany, oak, south-ern pine, and a dozen specialty woods would add to the flames like rare spices in a gourmet salad.

With the adjacent building less than a hundred feet away from His Mansion, the heat began to curl the wooden shakes on the side facing the fire. The roof shingles began to melt. His Mansion would burst into flames at any minute. A hu-man circle formed out on the front lawn, and everyone began to pray with fervency. Against all earthly hope, we prayed.

Meanwhile the fire trucks from six towns drew water from the Quinebaug River below and poured it on the burn-ing building. It was so hot that the water turned to steam, rose up into the air, and was caught by a breeze that shifted over His Mansion. The water condensed and rained down on the building. While the mansion next door burned to charred rubble, His Mansion suffered only minor damage. The fire-men said it was impossible. We believed it was a miracle.

When I arrived at the scene, the flames brought my flash-back to an end. The entire second floor was engulfed. There was no saving the place. There'd be no miracle today. The circumstances of the moment exceeded my faith and I was crushed. I broke down and vented my anger on God. Only the grief I experienced as a consequence of sinning against God, my wife, and others was more acute than that resulting from this new disaster.

Losing the grand old building itself was painful enough, but the destruction of the patina on a Stuben chandelier, that took a hundred years of gentle aging to produce, the loss of hand-carved mantles, interwoven oak latticework, and hand-tooled horsehide wallpaper, made it worse. These were things that could not be replaced. They embodied the character and mystique that made the grand building more than ordinary.

I was reminded that when moral integrity is breached and

I was reminded that when moral integrity is breached and when trust is broken the results are similar. There are things destroyed that cannot be replaced overnight. Only time and testing can rebuild flawed character and restore the patina of integrity.

Fortunately, not everything was consumed by flame thanks to volunteer firefighters from six surrounding communities. Once the embers were cold, the carcass of the stately Victorian was literally picked apart: mantles, fireplaces, circular staircases, beveled mirrors, light fixtures, oak flooring, and precious hardwoods.

"Who'll gimme a thirty, a thirty-five—who'll go fifty?" One after another the pieces--each a tag on some precious memory--were sold. The auctioneer was selling pieces of my life's journey to the highest bidder. This was a sad day, indeed. Hopes and dreams going up in flames evoked a question that had cried out in my heart years before when God's Spirit convicted me of sin, and repentance replaced denial: "Will there be a tomorrow--will God permit a second chance, a new beginning?"

* * *

Questions regarding the future were far more than theological; they had a very practical side. Camping out in the rectory of a nearby Episcopal Church got old fast. Each night the toys and furniture in the nursery were pushed aside and the contents of garbage bags--foam mats, and personal belongings--were emptied out. Everyone's clothing reeked of wet charcoal. Our nerves were frayed. If we stayed in this situation long, things would explode and our vision may wilt and die. Explaining a "sewage swimmer" to a social worker seemed like small potatoes in comparison to what we now faced.

The various camp and conference grounds I contacted could not accommodate us, especially during the winter months. In a last ditch effort, I called <u>Christian Herald</u> Magazine. Six months earlier they had offered to sell us their vacant conference center in New Hampshire, but their price was far too high. Perhaps if they heard our plight, they would let us rent it. After consulting with his board, Fenwick Loomer, Christian Herald's president, called with bad news.

One week later, Christian Herald's representative called back. "Was there *any* way we could extend an offer to purchase? Any offer?" Curious, I asked why the sudden urgency. Mr. Loomer shared that within days of my initial call three large well-known cults had expressed interest in the property. Christian Herald wanted to be able to truthfully tell the interested parties that they already had an offer to consider. Sale of this property had now become a matter of God's priority and preferences. Both parties could come out winners.

God put the deal over the edge. For us, the Christian Herald Board agreed to carry the paper at 6% interest. There was only one hitch: they needed to have the binder in hand before the end of business hours that day! With $25,000 in cash stuffed in a grocery bag, I raced to meet the deadline.

Christian Herald's office building was located just behind Reader's Digest in Pleasantville, New York where parking was impossible. It was 4:45 in the afternoon. I had no time to spare, so I double-parked the car and ran inside to find Fenwick Loomer's office.

Standing breathless in the mahogany-lined office, I realized that the sack filled with cash was still on the front seat of the car! My mad dash out to the car and back had to have set a record. Since I often leave keys in the ignition, it was a miracle that the car with its precious cargo was still there.

My second entrance found me better prepared. I placed the crumpled bag in the center of the massive boardroom table before three baffled and amused corporate executives. As the papers were signed, the loaves and fishes in my paper sack were transformed. They became a village on a hill, where God

92

would multiply in ways that far exceeded our imagination. Trusting Him for the details would be easier having witnessed His gracious provision.

To our good fortune, there were no zoning ordinances in the town where the vacant retreat facility was located. But having been raised on an island in a small community setting, I knew this would change quickly if it were known in advance that we were coming. We could expect no welcome wagon, but we did have a place to relocate. A strategy formed for transplanting the His Mansion family. Despite the disaster, the journey would go on. The dream, although altered, remained intact.

In the above examples people were hurt and disappointed, but good rose out of the ashes and lessons were learned. I wish I had answers and explanations for every calamity, but I do not. Unexplained, painful tragedies that no amount of human effort can fix have the potential to derail one's spiritual journey, however, those who pursue adventures of any significance should not always expect a smooth, level path. We will, at times, hit dead ends. What then?

*　*　*

"What the world needs now is love, sweet love." Poets and bards through the ages have sung the same song a thousand different ways. Each one's idea of how it can best be realized may be different, but the truth, the need for love remains the same. Likewise, those who seek to be loved and accepted in the His Mansion community are as diverse as history's minstrels.

Tom's life began in a poor African-American family that struggled to make it out of the rut of poverty and to get a piece of the American pie. More than anything else, Tom longed for love and acceptance.

Tom's dad was retired from the Navy and had settled in a nice house in a predominately white neighborhood. He worked hard to fit in and be a good neighbor. Most fathers place a certain amount of hope and expectation on their sons. Tom was his only son and this dad was no exception. Slight of build, Tom was not destined to be a great athlete and academically, he was not going to rival Galileo or become a brain surgeon. In fact, he was running well behind his birth certificate on the road to maturity. Tom craved attention and could sense the rejection, but he could not afford to alienate the only one whose acceptance might rescue him from obscurity.

Tom had heard his father regale him with stories of racial injustice--how whites and Jews controlled the system and would still keep slaves if the law allowed it. The evening paper gave daily evidence that the deck was stacked against blacks. Then, as if on cue, some evil bigot shot and killed the "King!" People who regarded Dr. Martin Luther's dream as their nightmare had silenced the man with a dream. Tom's hatred and anger found a target; "Black Power" supplied the ammunition. His denim jacket became a patchwork of sewn-on statements: "Power to the People," "Black Power," "Malcolm X--the new Savior."

Acceptance in this group involved more than Tom had bargained for. One night he lay unconscious in an alley from a drug overdose, while some form of pneumonia ravaged his lungs and immune system. A rare virus attacked his central nervous system, leaving Tom jerking and drooling. He gradually lost control of his hands and feet. His facial muscles became so unreliable that he could speak only one word at a time, and that with great difficulty.

The fact that he was a walking billboard for hate wasn't enough to earn acceptance. Tom had become repulsive even to his own "comrades." Realizing that no one was attracted to him, he retreated to his parent's home.

His father's shame was now justified. He insisted that Tom not leave the house during the day or in any way make himself obvious to the neighbors. The last thing he wanted was to be disqualified by some unexpected social faux pas.

Being incarcerated in his parents' home was more than Tom could bear. His outbursts and disruptive behavior became intolerable. A fledgling church that his mother attended heard of his plight and reached out to him. A man who attended the church encouraged his mother to allow Tom to go to His Mansion and the Samaritan volunteered to drive him there. The car drove up to the same portico at His Mansion, where President Roosevelt had once stepped out of his carriage during the mansion's former life. Tom emerged from the car and I mused on the vast irony embodied in this historic contrast.

Tom recognized me as the director and promptly saluted with an out-thrust arm and tightly closed fist. His decorated jacket clearly identified him even if his ensuing behavior had not. The revolutionary, fueled by a cesspool of seething anger, did all within his power to turn us against him. Hadn't his comrades shunned him and his dad not fully accepted him? But love is stronger than hatred and acceptance will drive rejection away. I don't remember when it happened, but the angry black soldier finally surrendered his sword and gave up his violence. Tom had learned to love us--accept us--without surrendering his "blackness." Badges of hate and division were removed from the street-worn denim jacket, revealing clean, dark-blue silhouettes.

Pursuing a relationship with Tom was not always an easy road to navigate. It required patience and an unusual level of compassion. Maureen secretly desired to hold a conversation with Tom, but was afraid she wouldn't understand him and would thus upset him. It was the handicapped who crossed the line first. "H..o..w c..o..m..e y..o..u n..e..v..e..r t..a..l..k t..o m..e?" Tom demanded in his painful staccato.

Maureen told him the truth. Tom bolted from his chair, returned with a pencil and paper and instructed her to have him write out what she didn't understand. "N..o..w, s..i..t d..o..w..n a..n..d t..a..l..k t..o m..e!" Thus began a unique brother-sister relationship.

At least once a month, His Mansion residents and staff visited surrounding churches, sharing stories of what God was doing in our lives. Old traditions and a fairly narrow view of religious conduct at church meetings, dominated a church that we visited one Sunday night. Having us inside their building was a stretch for them. But it was a Sunday evening meeting, which usually allowed a margin of flexibility.

The large number of young people up on the platform singing and talking made folks a bit uncomfortable to begin with. The fact that several members of our troupe were not familiar with the words of the songs and most couldn't hold a tune in a bushel basket didn't hamper our enthusiasm, but it did leave some spectators squirming. Riots were the order-of-the-day at nearby Yale University, and the sight of Tom, a peculiar-looking black fellow bounding up on the stage cranked the level of anxiety up several notches. Tom couldn't sing--it was difficult enough for him to speak--so once the beat had been established, he pulled out a police whistle which hung on a chain around his neck and blew "tweet-tweet-tweet" to the beat. He had everyone's attention--oh, yeah!

Several young men and women were scheduled to share their testimonies with the congregation and one by one they told their stories, and sang familiar hymns. The staid old folks began to feel more at ease and the congregation breathed a corporate sigh of relief. But blood pressures soared again, when the musician holding the first chair in the police whistle section approached the microphone. Everyone held their breath as their worst fears came to life.

The place was deathly still. The striking evangelist took what seemed forever to gain a grip on the microphone and compose himself. He sucked the drool and saliva from around his tongue and drew a deep breath in preparation for each individual word. Everyone agonized through the procedure with him while Tom formed the words, finally speaking them: "J e s u s . . . l o v e s . . . m e , t h i s . . . I . . . k n o w , for...the...Bible...tells...me...so!" Wiping his eyes, he stumbled back to his place. Perhaps a more powerful message has never been preached in that church.

Despite Tom's progress, his father was ill at ease with his son's acceptance in this newfound, predominantly white family. Yielding to his dad's strong influence, our beloved friend and brother left the community. Having finally tasted freedom and acceptance, Tom returned to an environment of tight control and social isolation because of a physical condition, that was a source of embarrassment to his father. The old lonely life at home was a far cry from the vitality and camaraderie the ex-revolutionary had come to enjoy.

It was Sunday morning and back in the His Mansion community, Tom would have been getting ready to go to church, but he was confined to his house. The only relief from his family prison was his old Pontiac still parked in the driveway. The engine still ran but it had no tires and was up on blocks. But more important than tires, the old bomb had a radio and the car served as Tom's refuge. With the comics section of the Hartford Courant Sunday paper in hand, he hobbled out the door to his "hiding place." The escapee attached the vacuum hose, started the engine, turned on the heater, and drove to his new home. Our comrade left us with little fanfare. News of his loss was hidden deep within the pages of a nondescript local paper.

*   *   *

In my years along the trail, I've laughed and rejoiced with fellow sojourners. I've shared the wonder of great discoveries and marveled at God's providence. The weak have gained strength, and the forlorn have smiled. But I've also witnessed a few wrecks along the way. Tom was only one of them.

Unlike Tom, who wanted to hate everyone else, Allie hated herself. She was raised in an upper-class home on Cape Cod. Allie's mom is an artist and Allie inherited her mom's gift. High school pictures revealed an unusually beautiful girl with everything going for her.

Mom and daughter arrived at His Mansion for an interview. Allie was a shrunken shell weighing eighty pounds. She had been in this condition before. Believing she was ugly and obese, Allie starved herself and purged anything she did eat. She had been given up for dead once already.

Once in the Mansion community, Allie responded to the love and discipline. Seven months later, everyone who remembered how she looked upon arrival could see an awesome transformation. It was in this transformed state that Allie entered my office and announced that she was going to quit the program. "I'm going home to die," she declared. When we were unable to persuade her to stay, her mom arrived to take her home.

Three months later, Allie lay in Yale New Haven Hospital with her electrolytes so low that her body refused to respond. She went into a coma and died. While with us, Allie wrote deeply profound poetry and painted pictures that inspired. She was a contributor--not a taker, beautiful, gifted, intelligent, and loved. Why did she give up?

Our lives have been enriched by the Toms and Allies who have journeyed with us. It is devastating when something like this happens and I have no simple answers or explanations for their loss. We do not comprehend why some crash and burn along the way. Although we grieve their loss, we dare not lose sight of the journey that lies ahead.

*   *   *

The older I get the more careful and reflective I become. I find myself purposely taking detours along the way that lead me back to the shore--to my roots. Even today, a favorite pastime of mine is to spend an hour or so shuffling along the beach at low tide. I'm searching for ornate pieces of building brick and fine china, delicate containers designed to hold perfumes and medicines, now polished pieces of every color. Things once fashioned and intended for specific purposes and roles. At first glance one quickly assumes that they are no longer of value, but this is not the case.

Now they lay hidden like small pieces of jewelry among the stones, broken shells, driftwood, and seaweed. Each one has spent thousands of days and nights making roundtrips to the ocean's edge amidst the pebbles and sand; inexorably worn and polished by the grit and pounding of everything they come in contact with. The potholes, parades, disasters, and deadends of life have a similar effect upon each one of us.

Out of the brokenness and distorted shards of human ideals emerge small rarities that stand out among the "rocks and rubbish" surrounding them. When moistened with Living Water they glisten and gleam--often resembling diamonds, rubies, emeralds, and sapphires.

Little children spend countless hours mysteriously entertained as they scour the sands and pebbles in search of these treasures. A jar filled with polished gems may be buried on an island--a map drawn and placed in a bottle and set adrift on the tide at summer's end. A buried treasure, indeed!

Life is sometimes like this. Our hopes and dreams--the expectation of others for our lives--shattered by some unexplained and unplanned "accident." The years following are filled with agitation and abrasions. Our fragile hearts are worn, chafed, and reshaped, all the while feeling as if we have been cast aside and no longer useful.

Years pass by, and should we surrender ourselves to the One who uses life's natural processes to shape us, we will emerge as finely polished gems ardently sought after by those who have cultivated an eye for the handiwork of the Divine Artist.

So it is with renewed zeal and keen focus that I search among the rocks and crevices as I pursue the upward climb, always blessed by the "precious gems" discovered along the way. In due time these treasures in jars of clay, shall also be gathered up, destined to adorn the crown of a king.

VII. COURAGE TO BEGIN AGAIN

False starts attack our resolve. "It's foolish to even think I could achieve anything worthwhile. Why make a fool out of myself? Maybe I should quit while I can." Such thinking signals impending surrender, and surrender brings the journey to an abrupt end. In contrast, C. S. Lewis said, "If only we have the will to walk, then God is pleased with our stumbles."* When we press on despite embarrassing falls and painful stumbles, it provides courage for others to take just one more step.

*Screwtape Letters, chapter 8

When all of our plans go up in smoke, it is easy to surrender or lose our way. Often those who have cheered us on, prayed, provided, and gave us the courage to continue. Gladys Griggs clearly remembers the 1979 phone call. "The Mansion has just burned!" the woman on the line said.

"It has? We'll have to see what we can do."

Gladys and her husband Harold acted quickly on the news. Many people brought clothing to help keep us warm, but Harold and Gladys were aware of another effect of being cold--one that could be satisfied only by filling the belly with something hot!

"I remember when I approached Stan," Harold explains. "I said, 'We're gonna bring you down a hot meal.' And he said, 'How are you gonna do that?' I didn't have that answer either."

"We didn't have much money, but the Lord's good," Gladys adds. When the Griggs got home, they decided to make beef stew. Their little cottage was heated by a small wood-fired cookstove, which also served to heat their house. The Griggs were willing and God would use what they had.

"We had a large kettle," Harold recalled. "And we borrowed a coffee urn from the church--a fifty-cup thing." For the next forty-five days the Griggs continued to be the channel of the Mansion's daily bread. Every noon they'd drive the thirty minutes from their home in East Putnam to Wauregan with a hot meal. Every evening at dark they'd return again with sandwiches. Their efforts enabled us to persevere.

We can learn so much from the way in which the Griggs live out their faith. Roughly twenty years after they began to follow Christ, they learned of the needs at His Mansion and did what they could to meet them. And so they gave. In fact, the last sacks of spuds donated by Harold and Gladys gained notoriety in the tragic Mansion fire. The *Norwich Bulletin* reported, "Strangely enough a pile of potatoes, part of the resident's food supply, lay in one corner, undamaged."

When folks like the Griggs are at your side, and you see their willingness to sacrifice to make you comfortable, the thought of quitting doesn't even enter your mind! Each year since then, on the evening before Thanksgiving, the His Mansion family is served a simple meal of peanuts, raisins, and oatmeal. It's a reminder of the days when that combination made up the menu for breakfast, lunch, and dinner, was welcomed and appreciated. After this annual memorial meal, Harold and Gladys' special role is retold, along with other stories of God's faithfulness through the years. The building where the Mansion family gathers today for daily meals, and where this unique annual feast is served, is aptly named "Griggs Hall."

The Griggs story gives us the hope that out of the ashes of defeat can come the victory of character and heart. Hopefully my own experience also attests to this.

* * *

My moral failure delivered a crippling blow to me-- and to Joan. I had failed in moral character and jeopardized my marriage and family. My conscience became my judge and found me guilty. Driving off during the night to some remote outpost, changing my name, and working as a laborer was appealing and thoughts of suicide occasionally sneaked into my consciousness.

Joan would certainly not been faulted had she walked through that open gate to begin life anew, taking Shawn and Sherree with her. Who would blame her? There were two alternatives available to her: Forgive and press on, or get out while the gettin' was good! Joan's commitment to God and what was in the best interest of our children won out in the end. I also won as a result of Joan's courageous choice.

103

In the aftermath of this failure, there was no way I could compound my sinful choice with yet another selfish decision. Abandoning loved ones by distance or willful death is the height of self-centeredness. Enough was enough!

During a season of remorse, God communicated to me that all the suffering, pain, and death that mattered had already taken place on a hill much higher that the one on which I knelt. It was time to accept His forgiveness, attempt to repair the damage, and move on.

Still reeling from my self-inflicted knockdown, the mansion's destruction by fire nearly sent me down for the count. This time it was a sense of responsibility and a desperate will to survive that motivated me to fight on. I had nearly ruined my marriage and the reputation of a great work only several years before this, and I was not about to quit because some adversary--seen or unseen--sought to destroy again. The warrior in me surfaced and I clearly sensed a source of Divine help and courage.

A hope that is more than a weak promise or empty encouragement from well-intended "wishers," is what sustains us through the worst of times. It is that still small voice of hope that whispers, "I will never leave you or forsake you," that spurs on the rally, which finally ends in triumph. God was, and is, the source of hope and Joan is the lens through which much of that light was focused.

Courage to begin again and the occasional victory can be the experience of every person no matter what their weakness or frailty. There are no travelers along the way who are outside the care and concern of the One who is aware of each and every sparrow that falls among the thorny thickets surrounding them!

*   *   *

Struggling fellow sojourners are particularly encouraged when the undeserving, unexpecting, ordinary casualty, finds strength to get up, shake the grit and dirt off, and sprint for the finish. Never, never, give up! Here are several vivid and inspiring examples of this truth in action.

Kevin Doyle stands among a group of forty men, women, and children gathered in a first-floor room of one of the two remaining houses in the Yugoslavian village that hasn't yet been bombed into rubble. The pungent smell of charred timber and cordite still assaults the senses even now. An older man translates for Kevin. The Kosovar refugees are eager to hear more about God and His Son. But a weariness and sadness also permeates the general mood. As they hear testimony of the love of God and of miracles performed by His Son Jesus, their minds involuntarily slide to memories of fathers, husbands, and sons who are no longer with them. Mass burial sites are being discovered every day and no matter how much they hope, they are certain a loved one rests in one of them. So they grieve over all.

It is only when Kevin loops the strap of his guitar over his head, that faces change--children first. His gifted fingers begin creating a flow of melody, harmony, and bass. Eyes fill with tears of relief and joy. Smiles transform faces that moments before were creased with despair--a testimony to man's innate drive to overcome and a tribute to the power of spirit-energized music!

When Kevin was thirteen his mom died and his angry, rebellious spirit had an excuse for full-blown revolution. New York City became his home-away-from-home and at fifteen he played music in local bars and occasionally traveled with a local band.

In the course of his involvement in the rock and roll culture, Kevin acquired a serious heroin addiction. During a California trip he went through withdrawal and nearly died

York City, but he continued downhill. With a heroin addiction and hepatitis B, Kevin became a regular at the methadone treatment center in Attleboro, Massachusetts, where he now performed in a local band. Because the hepatitis had gone untreated, Kevin was told he had six months to live.

There in Providence--the City of Life--Kevin Doyle was dying. He recalls standing on the corner of "Doyle and Hope Street," in Providence, and experiencing an encounter with "something," or someone unseen. Kevin describes this encounter as an "I love you," combined with a stern warning. I've personally visited this area and sure enough, there is such an intersection named Doyle and Hope Streets.

A Jewish convert to Christianity took Kevin, still addicted and suffering seizures, to a shelter at St. Patrick's Church. Another musician, John Polce, was a pastor in that church. There at the Christian community of St. Patrick's, Kevin had his second encounter with the mysterious guide, only now the guide had a name--Jesus!

Frank Gonzales was Kevin's roommate for two years at the community. Frank had recently benefited from spending time at a place of healing called His Mansion and strongly recommended to Kevin that he move there, which he did.

I welcomed Kevin--well, I met him at the door! He was a derelict. His hair was dirty, knotted, and long. His breath smelled as if it had just come from a funeral for his teeth. He looked as if he'd crawled out from under a rock! A staff person standing off to one side commented that Kevin bore stark resemblance to one of the characters in "Planet of the Apes." After Kevin consented to a haircut and a shower, I accepted him into the program.

Because of his eagerness to learn and serve, it wasn't long before Kevin was given responsibility. He had exceptional talent, and he began to travel with me, providing the music, when I went on outreaches to present to churches what

music, when I went on outreaches to present to churches what the fledgling healing community was all about.

During one such weekend outreach I taught two messages that, according to Kevin, had significant impact on his life. One was from Matthew11: 28-30, the passage where Jesus invites us to be yoked with Him as oxen are yoked together. Later that day we visited a farm and watched the farmer train a young ox to submit to a yoke. The farmer and his oxen provided an illustration for the message that I would never have been able to communicate as adequately with words.

The other message that impacted Kevin, was the story of Elijah and his self-exile in a cave and how God subsequently coaxed him out. God arrested Elijah's attention, not through powerful miracles and natural phenomena, but in a still small voice. Kevin wrote one of the most moving songs I've heard, based upon that message. Sunday afternoon, before we headed back to His Mansion, I baptized Kevin in the farmer's swimming pool.

Several weeks later, a friend called to say that Kevin's brother had either frozen to death, or been the victim of organized crime in Providence, a few nights before. Kevin and I went to the city morgue to identify the body. Kevin had tiptoed along the same ragged edge for years where his brother had now lost his footing.

Two weeks after absorbing this blow, while conducting an outreach at a Baptist church on Smith Hill in Providence, a young woman cornered Kevin: "Did you have a brother named 'JD'?" She went on to tell Kevin how she had spent time with JD in the park where he hung out, telling him about the love of Jesus. On the third occasion of their visits, JD responded and committed his life to Christ. The next day he either froze to death or was murdered. In any case, he completed his journey.

Not long after Kevin became a follower of Jesus, he remembers standing in front of a synagogue staring at the Star of David and feeling the fire of passion for the plight of the Jews in Israel. At that time he was completely unaware that his mother had been an Irish Jew. He now shared this burden for Israel with the leadership of the church that he attended. The older brothers recognized Kevin's immaturity and lack of qualifications and recommended that he acquire medical training before attempting such a venture. This would also give him time to grow in other areas.

Kevin was serving at the Mansion in Connecticut at the time of the fire. While Kevin and another staff person tried in vain to quell the flames the residents barely escaped with the clothes on their backs. Nearly everything was lost. In an act that held no heroics, as the front of the building was not yet engulfed, I scooted in and rescued Kevin's guitar from the mud room under the staircase. After the fire devastated the mansion in Connecticut, Kevin remained living in the carriage house for security until the mess was cleaned up and valuables auctioned off. That being finally accomplished, Kevin made the trek to our new location in New Hampshire. Soon afterward he began studies leading to qualification as an Emergency Medical Technician.

The leadership of a local church in New Hampshire became satisfied that Kevin now had the necessary tools and "commended" him to go to Israel and study the language and culture in preparation for serving there. While there on a Kibbutzim, Kevin worked and learned Hebrew. Later he taught Bible Studies in Haifa where he met Aliza, a Jewish woman who believed that Jesus was the Messiah. They married and soon after, Kevin joined the Israeli Army and served in Lebanon. Upon completion of his enlistment, Kevin returned to Israel where he took employment as the head of a unit of the Red Star of David, an emergency medical agency.

When Kevin returned to the United States several years later for additional education, he accepted a position on staff of a church in Massachusetts. When the breakup of the Soviet Union began, a colleague invited him to travel with him to Russia. The fix was in! Kevin's experience with Russian Jews in Tel Aviv and his fluency in Hebrew, paid rich dividends among the old-timers and young Russian Jews who seldom heard their own ancient language spoken by an American missionary. It gave him special credibility.

It wasn't long before Kevin was asked to oversee regular ministry to the refugees in Yugoslavia. The church where he now pastors has mobilized teams, and Kevin regularly travels with these teams to Kosovo, the Ukraine, and Russia, distributing money, medicine, clothing, and Bibles.

From the alleys and bars of New York City to a bombed-out village in Kosovo; from drug-drenched rock-and-roll to hymns of glory; from being a sick, homeless vagrant, to a healer, musician, and evangelist, Kevin's journey continues to inspire hope in timid, wounded travelers that he meets along the way.

Standing amidst the rubble and surrounded by widows and fatherless children, Kevin caresses the strings and for a few moments the sun shines and the birds sing. The Prince of Peace is replacing the Miloseviches of those ravaged nations. But wars are waged not only among nations, but also in the hearts of individuals. There can be little peace while such wars rage on.

* * *

There was a war raging in Linda's heart and absolutely no peace to be found. Her life was falling apart. She needed help and called His Mansion only to discover that the population there was in excess of thirty--way overfilled. In an effort to escape the people, places, and things that were her chains, she sought refuge working at an isolated dude ranch in Wyoming. The setting should have been invigorating but she was sick all the time.

"It's just altitude sickness," an old cook explained. "You'll get used to it." After a couple of weeks, the new ranch hand began to wonder, *How long does this altitude sickness last? 'Cause I seem to keep gettin' it every morning.* Two Wal-Mart test-kits convinced her of the answer.

The next morning she called her mom and dad and with both of them on the line she announced, "I'm pregnant." Just as she feared, there was silence. She was already in what seemed to be dangerous territory, so in a trembling voice, she ventured forth again and said, "I'm gonna have the baby."

"Praise God!" was her Dad's thoughtful response. Given Linda's well-established pro-choice stance, this decision to carry the child was not the response her mom expected--but God had intervened! Shortly after their conversation, her father flew out to Wyoming to drive home with his daughter. During the long ride home, Linda expressed concern about her mother's reaction. Each time her dad reassured her, as if he was aware of information that she was not aware of, "I think your mom's going to be a whole lot more understanding than you think."

When the prodigal daughter told her mom about the idea the old ranch cook put into her head--adoption--she didn't expect a positive response. But her mom told her a story. The plot paralleled Linda's experience, but the participants were different. The main character was Linda's mother, who at age eighteen had also entrusted her firstborn to other parents. This secret, kept for almost a quarter of a century, was revealed at an ordained moment.

After she had told her folks, Linda told her boyfriend (the father of the child), about her predicament. He gave her money to "take care of it." The plan sounded good and for a moment Linda was persuaded. But having grappled with God on the issue, she regrouped and made a new plan. Linda had heard about the special program for pregnant women in crisis, called New Beginnings, which had begun at His Mansion in 1984, but never thought it was going to play a role in her life. Now everything had changed. She called His Mansion again and learned that there were immediate openings at New Beginnings. She used the money her boyfriend had given to her for an abortion to buy a ticket to New Hampshire.

The problems that initially motivated Linda to call His Mansion were still there to be dealt with. Rebellion, anger, and bitterness energized her conflicts with staff and roommates. Forgiveness, not so much for her but by Linda for others, was the most crucial issue. "How could God possibly love me" was challenged in magnitude by "why should I ever forgive those who abused me?" Linda was being transformed--one day and one incident at a time.

Dealing with her emotional issues paled in comparison to the decision she faced regarding her child's future. "The morning my daughter was born, I felt like my whole world changed," Linda remembered. "I had no idea how I was going to follow through with the decision I had made to place my child for adoption." After three days together in the hospital, mom and daughter parted ways until mom was able to make up her mind. Could she follow through with letting others parent her child? More than a week passed. Peace was hard to come by and indecision reigned. But when Linda placed her daughter into her new mother's arms, peace flooded her soul.

Facing the consequences of years of earning a bad reputation is a tough uphill climb and getting caught and being confronted with our trespasses is never an enjoyable experience. It can feel like a serious setback, but often satisfaction throughout the remainder of our pilgrimage is enhanced by just such encounters.

*   *   *

111

The barking woke Carl from a sound sleep. The Chow and Labrador were at it again, as was the neighborhood Potcakes (the Bahamian version of the Heinz 57 variety). Peeking out of his upstairs window, Carl spied the cops. There was a familiar face among them, not a welcome one, a guy he knew from his days on the force. The electronic toys stashed in his room reminded him of the reason the cops were there. His conscience wasn't working well these days.

As the landlady let them in, Carl feigned sleep. Maybe they would just go away. His phony dream act was disturbed when he felt the cold steel muzzle of a 9mm Smith & Wesson pressed to the back of his head. The loot lying about his apartment left him with no excuse, so Nassau's Finest cuffed him and hauled him off to the station. There they beat him badly for an hour or so. He was tough, but the cigarette lighter in his face convinced him. Confession made, the abuse ended.

In his cell, Carl mused over the apparent futility of life. He replayed events that had brought him to this place. Years before, his cousin, head of the local police force, added qualifying inches to Carl's recorded height and much to his amazement, the high school dropout passed the police exams. Carl became one of the "good guys," but the uniform and training also made it easier to steal and deal. Over time he took the easy, more lucrative route.

When he was finally relieved of his duties, Carl became homeless. The beach became his bed and he called it home for years, even while attending welding school. He also continued to smoke crack, snort coke, and break the law. Life on the beach came to a stop in a jail cell. As he awaited his court date, a man talked to Carl about eternity. The coarse, rogue cop decided that he wanted heaven, not hell. As he says, "Nothing big happened. My cell did not shake and my body did not go numb. But Jesus came into this addict's heart!" Life for Carl was off to a new start.

No one came forward to press charges, and Carl was released from jail. Now a free man, Carl's resolve to live a new life held until the festivities of the Christmas season overwhelmed him. He slipped back into crack and burglary. He was back in court for burglary--appearances number four--but the plaintiff had a change of heart and dropped Carl's charges. The judge turned to his now familiar guest and said, "Mr. Cartwright, you are free to go, but if I ever see you in this courtroom again, I won't even hear your case. It'll be straight to jail."

Carl wanted to make a new start, but it took more courage and determination than he alone could muster. This was when Lew Gervais entered Carl's life. His Mansion had commissioned Lew Gervais and his family to serve as missionaries in the Bahamas where the drug problem was tearing the island-nation apart. Lew's challenge was to help establish a drug and alcohol program in Nassau. Carl and Lew connected.

Being married to a native Jamaican, Lew was privy to the age-old East Indian adage, "You scratch my back, I'll scratch yours." His Mansion in New Hampshire needed a welder, and Carl could use a change of scenery. Getting the U. S. Embassy excited about accepting a drug dealing, ex-cop felon into the country would be another hurdle. After three months of politicking--and lots of prayer--Carl headed north.

Initially, folks were quite leery of this moody character and Carl was as uncomfortable with the His Mansion family as some of them were with him. All this hugging, crying--and honesty! But others, such as Grandma Jean, the stereotypical "prim and proper" retired schoolteacher, were drawn to the rough-looking Bahamian. She thought Carl, with his trademark red bandanna around his head, resembled a pirate.

The "aggie foreman," Dean Winchell, became the tool God used to shape this welder. Although Carl modeled a work ethic that made him a leader among the guys, he still had much to learn. Dean taught him how to live an upright life as they shared lunches together. Carl was surprised by the way in which Dean demonstrated those principles throughout the day.

One step at a time, Carl built a new life. Today he is married, raising a family, and active in his local church. His relatives and friends back on his "family island" are amazed and encouraged by Carl's transformation. They recognized that marshaling the courage to fight against years of criminal behavior required energy and power outside of Carl.

It is one thing to get back up and start again when the fall was largely the result of your own doing. It is quite another when you are the victim of abuse that crushes, cripples, and disfigures. Being driven back to the starting line time after time tests the will.

* * *

A list of every act of physical and sexual abuse that Ingrid suffered fueled the flame of hatred and bitterness, which lead to chronic bingeing, purging, and other self-destructive behaviors. An incestuous assault resulted in an unwanted pregnancy that Ingrid subsequently aborted. The memory of this unspeakable abuse lay carefully pushed away into the recesses of her consciousness where it awaited a periodic unleashing provoked by some incident or piece of conversation. The freehand drawings Ingrid had made of the objects used by her oppressor in his torturous guessing games turned red, orange, and then black, as the purifying flames devoured them. Ingrid and her mentor, Joy, stood and watched, eyes fixed on the small piece of concrete where the fire burned. Tears. Disbelief. Ingrid's calculated choice to forgive was symbolized in a pile of white ashes.

Months of considering God's command and wrestling with her anger had preceded this moment--this giant step toward healing. Why should she forgive? He deserves, as she wrote at one point, to "go through a slow, methodical, painful...death." Ingrid even wanted to help it happen. But those steps were in the wrong direction on a destructive path. God wanted her to choose a different path. To do so, He commanded that she forgive this man. She wasn't completely sure why God would require this, but she was willing to trust Him. If she wanted a new destination, this was a necessary step.

After close observation and lots of questions, Ingrid had chosen a new direction for her life. She had entrusted herself to Someone who was, and is, bigger than she understood. But her decision didn't make life easier. The memories and nightmares still came, accompanied by disassociation and the tendency to fall asleep whenever she stood still. When she awoke from these trances, she'd be 13 again.

At one point, this setback seemed insurmountable. Four months into her stay at the Mansion, it was determined that Ingrid's needs exceeded the help that we were able to provide. She had to leave. She'd be welcome to return when she could remain in reality. The hurting woman left, expecting to be away for a couple of months. It was over a year later before it looked like she could return. But when she informed the staff that she desired to return, it was discovered that her dosages of medication exceeded our limits. She'd have to use a lower level of medication to keep from dissociating before we could follow through. Ingrid consulted her psychiatrist and learned that decreasing her medication would take at least a couple of months. Discouraged, she prayed.

"God, do I even need these meds? God, you're supposed to be bigger than anything, you're supposed to be more powerful than anything. That's what I've come to believe, that's what I'm standing on, ya know? God, I wanna just trust you that if I stop taking these tonight, you will take the place of them and you will do what they are doing."

God honored her prayer. Ingrid hasn't taken the medications since. Though she doesn't recommend this approach to others, in her desperate situation it seemed to be the only way. However, the physical ramifications of constantly purging food caught up with her and the acute abdominal pain persisted even when she kept her food down. Pepto-Bismol and prescriptions weren't cutting it.

What about prayer? Taking God's Word and their leadership roles seriously, three directors and Ingrid's interns, Beth and Joy, agreed to pray with Ingrid.

Eventually Ingrid admitted to others that during one prayer she felt a warm sensation start in her stomach, move up her torso, and gradually leave her body. Initially she remained silent. *"They'll think I'm crazy,"* she thought. But unable to keep her excitement to herself, she shared what had happened.

In time, Ingrid's internal pain shifted from the physical to the emotional. Questions tormented her. *Where was he now?* She didn't know how she could live with what she'd done to her aborted son of incest. *Where was he? Was he suffering in hell because he hadn't had the chance to choose Christ?* Answers came from many, but Ingrid still wasn't convinced.

Nightmares woke her again. Why sleep if nightmares are what you'll get when you do? Ingrid went into the living room to read. At 4:55a.m. on the morning of June 3, she found rest. Job, chapter 3, finally convinced her that her son was with Jesus.

For the next hour, she read and reread these verses: "Why did I not perish at birth and die as I came from the womb?...For now I would be lying down in peace; I would be asleep and at rest with kings and counselors of the earth...Or why was I not hidden in the ground like a stillborn child, like an infant who never saw the light of day?...there the weary are at rest...the small and the great are there."

"I must have read these verses 20-25 times," she recalls, "People weren't just telling me [that my son was safe], *God* was telling me."

Despite this assurance, her grieving continued. Ingrid realized that the memory of her son had taken on an unhealthy dimension. She knew she must let him go and trust in God's grace.

Weeks later while standing on the rocky North Atlantic shoreline, as the waves pounded and retreated, the idea came in powerful clarity: *If God made this, then He can certainly take care of my son.* Again the thought came: *The God who created this vast ocean, this beauty, is taking care of my son.* The waves thundered on the rocks and took the responsibility for the unborn son's care to the God of all comfort as the tide receded into the ocean.

Other troubled and tortured souls, having suffered as Ingrid suffered, have followed her up the hill to healing. Ingrid has returned to His Mansion to offer hope and comfort to young women who have passed over the same rough territory that she has. As they watch her overcome, they catch a view of her source of strength and gain the courage to make their own upward climb.

* * *

Ingrid's example serves as a tab on the file of my own experience as well. Several years ago I took my "baby brother," Jeremy, eight years my junior, out on *Fenian's Rainbow,* a lobster boat that I keep on the coast of Maine. Jeremy and I have spent little time together because he was only nine years old when I left home to join the Navy. So while on *Rainbow* we talked of our childhood. I shared, among other things, about how our neighbor had molested me before we left the island.

At this point, Jeremy's eyes filled with tears, "O my God!" The older guy who had abused me must have initiated his own younger brother, because his younger brother had in turn abused Jeremy!

* * *

117

Unless the traveler is optimistic enough to believe that the road will get better it is understandable that they may conclude that life is the pits, given the craziness of the world we live in. Fortunately, each person <u>can</u> make a difference. It is possible to make the road ahead more safe and straighter.

We must gather our resolve and continue on, individually as it is with communities. His Mansion was no exception. A month and a half after the magnificent Victorian burned down, the refugees from the rectory gathered for final prayer and farewells. No one quite knew what lay ahead, but everyone stepped forward.

We resembled the Boers trekking across the South African Transvaal--in more ways than one! Inside the van was a pregnant cow, which we hoped would be the beginning of a small herd, and trailer full of pigs. Fortunately, we had no goats or chickens!

On February 27, 1979, under the cowardly cover of darkness, we took a courageous step toward a new beginning. A dilapidated, green van carrying animals, a truck loaded with our meager belongings, and several barely respectable automobiles filled with a dozen courageous veterans who elected to continue the journey, wound their way north to our new home in the hills of New Hampshire.

When we arrived at the town green in the center of Deering, less than a mile from our new home, the van containing the four-legged pregnant lady gave up the ghost. A young man, barely twenty, was in charge of the convoy and made an executive decision. He would lead the cow down the middle of Rte. 149. It was a good thing we had chosen a nighttime operation or our stealthy occupation of a key piece of Deering real estate would have been exposed.

By daylight, snow had covered our tracks. The life and vitality of two dozen young men and women filled with hope and inspiration acted like a defibrillator. The empty village on the hillside came to life! His Mansion's family had moved to its new home. Like the seeds saved from last season's harvest, this community would bloom once more.

VIII. FORDING RIVERS/CROSSING CANYONS

In the course of life's spiritual journey we will also encounter challenging impasses. Personal failures, unexpected losses, bad advice, and heartbreaking disappointments may appear as raging rivers and deep canyons on our life's landscape. Pressing on may seem impossible, yet God expects us to do the possible and divine help awaits our plea to conquer the impossible.

Fenian's Rainbow loafed along at seven knots, picking its way through a maze of cuts and channels as our friends and co-workers Lee and Joyce Oliver and I exited Muscongus Bay. Finally, in the open water of the large bay, I plotted a course toward Loud's Island where our cruising guide indicated an Audubon bird sanctuary was located.

Seaward from Loud's Island, we spotted two figures standing in a de-masted vintage Cat boat frantically waving their arms. As the distance closed between us I could see the mast had been intentionally removed and the boat relied upon a diesel engine, except at this moment, the engine was dead. A seventy-year-old woman casually dressed in baggy pants and an oversized work shirt was the skipper of the craft. There were two other adults and a child with her. The not-so-trusty Perkins diesel had stalled and now refused to start. Lee, a retired Coast Guard Engineer, determined that the injectors were air-bound, but an attempt to purge them only worked temporarily. Without power the prevailing currents were carrying the boat out to sea. Unsuccessful at repairs, I volunteered to tow the powerless craft home.

The lady captain said she had a mooring across the narrows which separated the mainland from the Hog Island Audubon reserve. When I told her where we were heading and what our cruising guide said, she laughed. "That book is famous for its inaccuracies. You should have a copy of Taft's *New England Cruising Guide*." Right! At forty bucks I ought to have a lot of things.

We towed them to her mooring, moored our own boat at Hog Island, and went ashore. Upon returning I spied a hardcover edition of Taft's book lying on the chart table. It was signed by both Mr. and Mrs. Taft and was dedicated to its previous owner, Betsy Noyce. Mrs. Noyce had inscribed a "thank you" under Taft's inscription, for rescuing us. What a wonderful gift!

Later that evening, as we chatted with Ralph and Gertrude Hoffses, whose family name graced the charts identifying the peninsula on which our cabin was located, I related our day's adventure. Our hosts were intrigued with our story and asked if they could look at the book. It was then that I learned the woman we had rescued was the wealthiest woman in the State of Maine. Her husband was the inventor of the "UPC Bar Code," used to price everything in the world!

With no power and a missing mast, the wealthiest woman in Maine had been helplessly drifting out to sea. Mrs. Noyce was dependent on a power outside of herself for safe passage home and finally had to wave her arms in the universal distress signal, just as any other unfortunate person would do. Somewhere on the journey through life we will inevitably be confronted with obstacles and situations that are beyond our control. Truth be known, for many of us it's not until we are confronted with the apparently insurmountable that God even becomes an option.

* * *

Matt Kantrowitz certainly discovered this to be true. Matt started out as a pampered, rich Jewish kid whose program for life included a stop at Brown University en route to a partnership in the family Law firm. The best laid plans of mice and men, as they say!

"Go ahead, jump. You've ruined your life," said a strong voice in his mind. "You had so much opportunity. You were in a good school. You're from a good family. Everything was laid out on the table for you, and you blew it. Your mind is fried now. You can't stop--won't stop--getting high. You might as well end the misery now. Go ahead, jump."

Matt tried to convince his counselors and peers of the possibility that he wasn't really responsible for what he did--sort of the "devil made me do it" con job.

"We don't want to hear your excuses," reported a staff member at the state-sponsored drug rehabilitation program. The laughing and mocking of his peers grew louder. This public shaming ritual was his punishment for getting high again.

"Well, I don't need this..." Matt answered as he turned over the table behind him.

"They thought they had me where I would just cringe and submit to their abuse," Matt remembers, "but I was too proud for that."

Project Renaissance, a state-sponsored drug and alcohol treatment facility situated on property adjacent to His Mansion immediately sent him packing. It didn't matter that it was the middle of the night. Matt found himself standing on rural Route 12. He didn't know which direction led home, so he decided to go next door. "I knew there were Christians there and thought, *They'll be charitable, they'll let me stay the night...then I'll figure out in the morning what to do with the rest of my life.*"

At 1:00 a.m. on April 11, 1973, the young Jew knocked on His Mansion's front door. The growling of an angry German Shepherd didn't do much to settle Matt's nerves, but houseparent Joe Wagner's large-hearted welcome soon allayed his fear. Matt explained his situation to this older man and was allowed to stay--on one condition: that he call his parents to tell them that he wasn't able to get back into the rehab center next door.

"After I made that phone call, I put my head on the desk and just cried." Tears still flow twenty-five years later as Matt describes the incident.

"As I wept, Joe Wagner--this guy I'd dragged out of bed--approached. Why should he have any regard for me? But he just gave me a really nice hug. In a sense I think my life as a Christian began then. I was up all night. I couldn't sleep. I was in turmoil."

A week later during lunch, Joe and several of the residents were discussing how one could become a member of God's family. Afterward, in the family room, Isabelle Wagner challenged Matt to put all of his guilt, shame, and failure in a package and leave it at the foot of the cross. Matt recalls, "We started to pray and, ah," he presses his thumb and forefinger against his eyes to dam the tears, "and I felt like I needed to do something more symbolic.

"I fell back on a synagogue ritual for the Day of Atonement. On Yom Kippur, there's a point at which the rabbi, on behalf of the whole congregation, prostrates himself in repentance before God. He literally lies down on the altar in the synagogue. So I lay down on the ground and prostrated myself before God's Son. I prayed to leave my burden at the cross. I accepted Jesus as God's Messiah."

During the next six months, Matt's mind was being restored--through one-on-one basketball games, reading Scripture, and being with other Christians. Every morning he sneaked into the mudroom beneath the stairs and prayed, "Lord, make me your servant." That he was changing became evident as Matt's extreme self-centeredness gradually gave way to a concern for others. But at times he relapsed into his old egocentricity and paranoia.

One morning, I heard screams coming from the bathroom upstairs--the women's bathroom--but the voice that caught my attention was a baritone--distinctly male! The soprano section soon drowned out the single male voice. Several of us attempted to open one, then another, of the three bathroom doors, only to discover each one had been locked from the inside.

"They're mine!" bellowed the male voice. "God gave them to me for my harem!" It was Matt, and he was determined to hold on to his bevy of frightened and unwilling captives. We forced open the door and rescued the damsels in distress. They were no worse for the wear and had an experience that they may, or may not, wish to tell to their children and grandchildren.

During his stay, Matt's girlfriend visited him with the intent of ending their relationship. But while visiting she also became a follower of Jesus Christ. In October of that year, I performed their marriage in the alcove of the family dining room and the Kantrowitzs began life as a couple. Within the year, the newlyweds had their first child.

But they still had some deep waters to go through. The proud father still had bouts with drugs every two-to-three months during their daughter's first four years. When he was straight, Matt read Scripture and was interested in his spiritual life, but the episodes of drug abuse still came. In addition to snorting money that was intended for necessities, up his nose, Matt was absent as a husband and father. His wife, like many who are married to addicts, lived in a terrified, anxious state.

In 1977, Matt was delivered from drugs. God met Matt at a canyon in his life. Desperate for help, Matt cried out and an Episcopal priest prayed for him. Matt explains, "I felt something unclean come out of me." He felt God calling him to a life of service and his home church put Matt, now a father of three, through seminary.

Matt's field requirements brought him to the Massachusetts State Prison in Walpole. He had no intention of doing prison work when he began his studies at Gordon-Conwell Theological Seminary, but he found himself feeling comfortable in the environment. For most New Englanders, the words comfortable and *Walpole* are antithetical. Walpole's climate can be compared to that of Attica or SingSing. During Matt's internship, the prison averaged a murder a month.

The contrast between his upbringing and his new environment was obvious, yet Matt was at ease. "I began to think about my own background and realized that I was no different from these guys. I was able to go onto the cellblock and feel comfortable. So the Lord confirmed right away that I should be a prison chaplain."

His mentor in the prison moved on unexpectedly, and Matt was left as the "defacto chaplain." After graduating from seminary, he became Protestant Chaplain at the State Prison in Thomaston, Maine. For twenty years he has attempted to build the type of community he experienced at His Mansion, among men doing "ten-to-life."

Today, some townspeople in Thomaston, Maine who volunteer in the prison, do so because they can't find the same sense of community on the outside. Matt works to raise men up who will be leaders in their churches after they are released. It's a concept that others have said cannot be done, but Matt learned long ago that it is in the "impossible" that God does His best work.

*　*　*

I, like Matt, have also witnessed a number of occasions in which there appeared to be no hope. Yet the river was crossed and the chasm was bridged.

While the distance across the gap may measure the same, it's the circumstances facing each individual that makes each crossing unique. Matt's choices created his own perilous plight, but sometimes things are not so clear cut.

Ann also faced a leap of faith, but her enemy seemed to be one of those dark, sinister monsters of which we know little and understand even less.

"In...the...n, nnn, name," unable to get it out, Ann threw her head against the wall. She hated the voices and the messages they shouted.

"Try again, 'In the name of Jesus, go away'," her intern coaxed. It was the only means Kelly knew to help Ann through

127

the crisis. She had already slammed her head into the wall six times. It was amazing that there wasn't a hole in the sheetrock and that her head still seemed unharmed.

The pain dulled the volume of the voices, but when she began to command them to leave, the voices grew even louder. "In the...n-n-naaa-me of J-e-e," her teeth seemed glued as she tried to get it out. "J, Juh, Jeee-sus..." Yes!

"Keep going," Kelly pleaded. In many of Ann's attempts, she was unable to get out the name of her Lord. But now she'd made it over that hurdle. This was no time to give up.

Ann's face was a deep red. Every pore on her head dripped sweat as she gasped for air. She continued, "G-gg-go..."

Kelly wouldn't act on Ann's behalf. She'd tried that already, but to no avail. Straining to hear any response Ann would make, Kelly repeated the directive in her mind hoping that Ann would get it.

"G-go a-a-aaaw," Ann cried in agony as she grabbed the hair near her temples, pulled, and threw her head into the wall again.

Defeat. Words of instruction and prayers from colleagues around the hill wouldn't bring relief this time. Something was very wrong. After more than forty-five minutes, Kelly phoned for Jim, the healing community's resident Bible teacher.

Jim arrived at the dorm and talked with the sweat-drenched woman who was still being assaulted by voices. He asked her about grace and they talked about Jesus. Instead of encouraging the repetition of rote phrases, he reminded her of the snake Moses held up in the wilderness. Jim then offered a simple challenge: "Look to Jesus and live." She responded. Ann lifted her eyes toward a power beyond her own--a power that would enable her to live.

In the midst of this crucial engagement, Ann fell asleep. If she wouldn't hurt herself in obedience to the familiar voices, then they would keep her from hearing any challenge to their authority. Kelly nudged her until she awakened and in minutes Ann was "back." The fear-inspired, darting glances were gone from her eyes. Looking around, her furrowed eyebrows seemed to ask how she got there.

It's a mystery, even for those who were there. One minute her physical safety is threatened by self-destruction (or self-defense); the next, all she has is a headache. What happened? Why didn't the words work? That's how we'd done it before, or so it seemed. Had the words lost their power? We've learned that it's not a matter of *how* you say it, or even *what* you say. The power is in *whom* we place our trust. It didn't matter what Ann heard, what mattered was to whom she looked. Looking to Jesus, the foundation of her faith, Ann experienced a peace that defied explanation. She had crossed over the chasm and was headed once again toward a life of freedom and purpose.

* * *

Amy, a veteran member of His Mansion's healing community, is convinced God has heavenly helpers assigned to help achieve the impossible. Angels are very much in vogue these days, but popularizing them for mere entertainment's sake has trivialized their genuineness and purpose. They are our invisible--and sometimes not so invisible--companions more often than we are aware. Amy is convinced that these heavenly chauffeurs might even be licensed to drive vans! She never saw her driver, but she recognized His power at work nonetheless.

"We don't have any brakes," Amy whispered to the woman riding shotgun with her, hoping that the other thirteen passengers wouldn't hear. She knew that the brakes were failing. The van slowed enough to hold for two red lights, but her attempt to stop at an upcoming gas station revealed that she had gone from some to none!

The van was rapidly approaching the next corner and just before Amy broke the law, the light turned. The green arrow pointing right prompted silent gratitude from the driver and her confidant. There was no time to celebrate, though. Three cars idled in the lane ahead of them less than a block away, waiting for a green light. If they only knew what was coming from behind. A timely light change--another reprieve!

The uphill grade gave the false sense of being in control, but on the slope gravity dominated. A turn would be impossible. Prayer and adrenaline peaked again. The only hope was a large parking lot separated by two lanes of traffic passing in both directions on the "Red Sea," known this evening as Route 202. Not until they actually penetrated the lane did a gap appear. But the miracle didn't end there. Once across, a slight incline slowed them down enough for Amy to jam the van into "park."

"What'd we hit?" asked protected passengers. Only then did they learn that they'd been without brakes for blocks.

The community's other fifteen-passenger van, christened The Ark, was miles ahead on its journey home and would not arrive at the mansion for another hour. The brakeless vehicle and its passengers were stranded. A call to the Mansion alerted the staff to turn the van around for a rescue, as soon as it arrived.

With seventeen people shoehorned into the rescue van, they headed home. Thirty minutes later, those who were still awake could smell the sweet, smoky stench that signals a toasted transmission. Four miles from its mountaintop destination the taxed and worn-out tranny became history. But the same Unseen Navigator who had guided and protected during the "free wheeling" trip earlier that evening, docked the Ark in front of the women's dorm. An unseen guide had, indeed, led them safely through treacherous waters.

While forging the tumultuous rock-strewn rivers of life, there are situations where it seems the only thing that keeps people afloat are the prayers of folks who love them. The power of prayer can rebuild bridges across deep chasms even before we reach them. Minni's story illustrates this truth.

* * *

Minni had returned to the healing community on the hill. Since leaving His Mansion nine years before, her life had been marked by chronic relapse. Lithium, Depakote, Paxil, and more. Prescriptions were easier to pick up than jobs--at least the honest ones. Detox, relapse--the cycle was getting old. Minni came only for food and shelter. That was reason enough for a time, but not for very long. Less than two months into her stay, she announced in a fury that she wanted to leave. She was feeling healthier and had grown tired of roommates and restrictions. She had enough.

Gail, her mentor, was concerned enough to challenge Minni. "All your life you've been chasing after things of the world," she said. "You've looked to drugs, you've looked to money, you've looked to sex, and everything has failed you. Isn't it time you gave God a chance?"

The question struck home. Earlier in life, Minni had professed to be a Christian, but her life-style didn't coincide. It was time to place her trust in a "power higher than herself" and make the leap to a new beginning.

Sometime later Minni read, "When you come to worship God and there is something between you and a brother..." the words gripped her, "...you must go first and be reconciled and then come and leave your gift at the altar." She knew what she needed to do. She wrote a letter to her brother, Raphael.

A week later Minni received a letter from Raphael with a note scribbled on the back of the envelope: "You and I must be praying about the same thing." Her brother had collected the letter from Minni as he was preparing to slip a letter to his sister into the "OUT OF TOWN" slot. Minni couldn't believe it. God had specifically and uniquely acted on her behalf.

As the date for Minni's completion of the program approached, she made plans to return to Florida. Not all of her trusted friends felt comfortable with this and suggested alternatives. Her strong will desired to resist their advice, but the "coincidence" of the crossing letters served to admonish her to let God direct the next step. Instead, she prayed and waited.

The next day, a nearby missions organization called and informed Minni of an opening. Minni was able to remain in the same housing, near a network of people who knew her. Over time, her employers entrusted this former thief with a key to every office in the building and gave her responsibility for financial accounts. Certainly, God had prepared the way.

Minni has learned the pattern. God takes care of her in ways for which He alone can claim the credit. This former addict, alcoholic, and prostitute knows there's a link between her obedience and God's provision. She also knows that running in the background--even when she was still resisting-- were the fervent prayers of her mother.

Minni came into her mom's room more than once while growing up, only to find her kneeling there praying. One night, when Minni came in at 2 a.m., she met her mom in the living room.

Immediately, her mom asked, "What happened?"

"Whad'ya mean?" she drawled. Minni was drunk.

Awakened in the night, her mom felt compelled to pray for her daughter. Minni had an accident on the way home and had totaled her car.

Minni once said that the letter from her brother was the first time she "saw God move." The persistent prayers of a mother and the love of a patient Father, however, revealed that it was simply the first time Minni noticed.

*   *   *

Arriving at that place where you have no more reserves or resources can be scary, but it is also in these places that our faith is strengthened. Crisis situations can be the oasis at which the thirst for purpose, courage, and hope may be quenched. A gentle nudge from God should be sufficient, but sometimes it takes getting hit by a house!

We received the call from the modular home manufacturer: "We'd like to bring the modular up next Tuesday." *Gulp!* Even though we didn't know how it would work out, we took a step of faith.

"Okay, we'll be waiting," I answered. The wheels were literally set in motion.

When I learned that the driver had been given the go-ahead, I realized that we had passed the point of no return. Sometimes, just sometimes, I wish acting in faith didn't feel so foolish. This is definitely a time I would have used one of my three allotted passes, if life had such luxuries.

Our long-term families needed space and this seemed like good timing as a donor well known to us, traditionally sent a substantial annual gift in mid-fall. In 1985 we allocated the anticipated gift in advance and ordered the modular home to be delivered fifteen days after the anticipated contribution's regular debut. That would leave enough time for the check to clear both banks before we cut the check to the builder.

Less than a week before the delivery, the donation had not materialized. The staff at His Mansion knew we needed $25,000 so they prayed eagerly--expectantly. We knew God would provide. He had before, and we trusted Him to do so now because we lacked the amount due. If we failed to present "payment in full" when the house arrived, the truck would turn around without unloading. Continental Homes never went back on its word!

D-Day, literally "Delivery Day," arrived, but the funds had not. Continental Homes called to let us know they'd be a day late. "No problem!" we replied. There would be no strain on customer satisfaction from that news!

But the next day, as predawn darkness gave way to a faint light, I knew that the day would begin without the large gift from our annual donor. It was a new day, a house was headed in our direction, and there wasn't enough to pay the deliveryman. It's one thing if it's just the oilman, but this was a house! There was no way I could tell the driver to go back. Doug and Betty Henderson, who had been living for months in a little camp trailer while awaiting housing, were already shouting, "Free at last, free at last!"

Like a boy expecting a "secret ring" in the mail, I waited nervously for the receptionist to return with the day's mail. No one likes to have someone hanging over his or her shoulder while they work, but there I was. Most of the return addresses brought faces and churches to mind, but not the one I anticipated. The wind out of my sails, I began to open the other letters. My heart sank as I concluded that this would not be a fun day.

Memories of the days that mortgage payments were due, and power shut-offs were threatened flooded my mind but the contents of good ol' P. O. Box 256, in Wauregan, Connecticut, saving the day flooded my mind. It was P. O. Box 40 in Hillsboro, New Hampshire's turn now. Even as I reminisced about our past needs and God's faithful promises, the next envelope produced a check for $25,000 from a donor we hadn't even considered. Talk about making the adrenaline pump!

We weren't over the canyon yet. I realized that the driver would not accept the donor's personal check--even if co-signed. He required a bank check. I was off in a cloud of dust. There was no Dunkin' Donuts in town in those days, so who knows where the local "black and whites" were hanging out. They certainly were not on my route to the bank.

Meanwhile, a staff member stood at the fork in the road at the entrance to our mountainside campus. While he waited to meet the truck, he polished his stalling tactics! They weren't needed, because as the truck with our new "house" behind it came rumbling up the private driveway, I came flying up the town road with the bank check in hand. I arrived at the junction just before the truck arrived and handed off the check to the waiting staffer as if it were a baton in a relay race. The check passed from his left hand to his right and into the truck driver's hand!

This is the kind of faith that makes you sweat! God knew exactly when we needed the money and He delivered "at the appointed time." I am particularly humbled by this story because I had placed a phone call after I had called the community together to pray for God's provision. The businessman in me didn't want to look foolish, so I had meddled. Truth be known, my phone call had secured a "hedge" to cover our obligation should our prayers not be answered. Time would mark this as a lack of faith on my part, but God is too big to be hindered by my small faith!

*　*　*

Filtered through steam rising from a piping-hot mug of Earl Gray, I studied the flames dancing in the 250-year-old fireplace. There's drama and movement between the vapor and flame that has yet to be captured even on the best canvases. The hypnotic interplay between flame and wood has always relaxed me. But on this night, the pounding on my door shattered my thoughtful reverie.

"Call 911. Call 911. The chapel's on fire!"

For Tom, the duty "stoker" for the evening, the nearest he had ever came to working with a heating system prior to his internship at His Mansion, was adjusting the environmental controls on his father's luxury sedan. Lacking experience

135

with wood furnaces, he had overfilled the unit and left the air intake wide open. The superheated condition melted the firewall between the primary chamber and the hot air ducts. Flames rushed into the church building as if it were the chimney.

News of the event spread as quickly as the blaze itself. All over the hill, those who were not physically fighting the fire with water fought it with prayer.

It was mid-January, the temperature was below freezing, and the water supply was limited. As the high ceiling of the chapel filled with heat and gases, walls of the newly constructed classroom/gym complex, which was attached, began to smolder. As hard as they'd fought, the firefighters announced that the entire building would be lost. Not comfortable waiting any longer, the fire chief issued the command: "Pull out. She's gonna blow!"

At precisely that moment, a hole opened in the roof of the chapel, sucking the heat and flames back from the walls and windows, venting them into the sky. On the side of a mountain where a stiff breeze is a constant, the open flames could have created another even more serious problem. But at that moment the air outside was still. The flames leapt straight into the dark sky, leaving the gymnasium and educational building uncharred.

Smoke saturated the walls of the building and students and staff scrubbed, scrubbed, and scrubbed again until only a nose with an agenda could detect the lingering lesson. A year later, a new chapel stood on the footprint of the old, and a two-storied educational facility bridged the gap between the new chapel and the gymnasium. God delights in bringing new life out of ashes!

As magnificent--perhaps miraculous--as these testimonies are, there are crises and catastrophes in life that seem to defy explanation, and tax our hope for resolution. In these situations we must look beyond ourselves. As deep and perilous as the chasm may appear to the traveler poised on the brink, we know there is One who would not have us dashed against the stones. It is not foolhardy to step into thin air when your trust is in the God of the impossible.

*　*　*

The mind is complicated and often mysterious. It has the capability of playing tricks--sometimes amusing and sometimes not at all. I remember an incident in my childhood that reminds me just how quickly our minds and imaginations can race out of control.

It was a typical hot summer evening, when the late setting sun tricks growing children into thinking that it is still early. I had been sent off to bed just when the island nightlife was cranking up. The salty semitropical air was filled with music, laughter, the sharp crack of rifle fire coming from the "shooting gallery," and the sound of candlepins being smashed by hand-sized bowling balls. If I were not permitted to participate in the revelry, I would certainly let my imagination out to play!

Lying in bed, I stared idly at the rough pine ceiling above me. The smell of the heated pine was soft, soothing, almost intoxicating. My restlessness subsided and I entered that semi-dream state that precedes sleep. I continued to stare. The sawyer who had cut the logs had sawn one plank right through a constellation of knots so that they splayed out like petals on a daisy. Years of curing had created cracks and fissures in the knots. A particularly interesting cluster of knots caught my attention--and sparked my imagination.

Two of the knots looked like eyes--tiger's eyes! Of course! I could see nostrils, brown and yellow stripes, the mouth with its fierce teeth. My heartbeat increased. On one hand I was getting sleepy, on the other I couldn't shut off my overactive imagination. I thought I saw his whiskers twitching. Yes, the tiger was coming alive!

The adrenaline level shot up. The ferocious tiger grinned at me. His teeth grew bigger and his ears tensed. He was about to attack! Before my rational mind (assuming I had one at that age) could regain control, I involuntarily screamed out in fear as the tiger slinked harmlessly away.

Unfortunately, the tiger occasionally comes to life and does ravish its victims. Kathy, a former His Mansion resident, had decided that being a human being held far too many risks. In a distorted and twisted moment, she thought, *"Anyone who commits a violent crime is un-human."* This led to the further conclusion that, *"If I commit a violent crime, then I'll be un-human and nobody will be able to hurt me anymore."*

Although she was way off base from an outsider's point of view, the protection of not being human was appealing. Her dad had abused her. Her grandpa, too. Her mother's response? "Don't make a mountain out of a mole hill." Yes, becoming un-human could be a good thing.

Kathy began to think constantly about committing a violent crime. Her cues were everywhere--newspaper articles, TV shows. There is a proverb in Scripture that states, "As a man thinks, so he is." She had screamed for help, too, but not before her mind had fulfilled its bizarre fantasy. Her tiger had really come to life!

Before Kathy's living nightmare, she had been a Student at His Mansion, but had left the program before her commitment was up. Her relatives had requested her help, and against our better judgment, she returned home. Soon her "stinking thinking" also returned.

Several months after leaving the program, Kathy put a butcher's knife in her back pocket and set out to become un-human. With each potential victim she approached, she couldn't bring herself to do it. A voice in her head taunted, "What's the matter? Can't you do *anything* right?"

138

The thought of hurting her brother's children had shot through her mind before, but she had always stopped short of acting on it and each time perceived herself to have "failed again." This time she would not listen to any internal warnings, she would succeed. As if she were a third-party witness, Kathy "observed" herself murdering her eight-year-old niece. Shocked that her fantasy had come to life, Kathy ran, convinced she could ditch the cops. On the well-worn path she followed through a stretch of woods, reality hit. Horrified, she hurried to a convenience store and told the cashier, "Someone needs to call the police. I just killed my niece."

"You're crazy," the employee replied.

"I'm serious. Someone needs to call the police. My niece has been killed."

"If you want to call, there's a pay phone right over there."

Kathy called and reported the crime, including details of how it was committed. The person on the phone asked, "How do you know all this?"

"Because I killed her."

"Can you wait right there until someone picks you up?" and Kathy agreed.

A squad car escorted Kathy to the scene and the niece was taken away by ambulance. The officer then asked Kathy for a statement. Her response was simple: "I did it."

The little girl died three days later.

At hearing the news everyone at His Mansion grieved, wept, and wondered aloud. No one who had any involvement with Kathy seemed free from the heart-wrenching question, "Could I have made a difference?"

In what we thought would be a last-ditch effort to make a difference in Kathy's life, two of the women who had worked with Kathy joined me in a visit to the county jail. Sixteen years later, on another visit, what Kathy shared surprised me. "I'll always remember one thing you told me. 'All of us have done things that we're not proud of.'" While this was true, I knew it would take a measure of grace beyond my natural human capacity, to forgive such a horrible deed.

It seemed to Kathy that her life ended when the metal doors clanged shut behind her and she faced the possibility of spending the remainder of her life in a horrible cage. In fact, Kathy's life was about to begin anew. A year into her twenty-to-life sentence, a fellow inmate named Kelly, began asking Kathy to come to church with her. Kathy couldn't stand being near people who were praying or reading the Bible. After eleven years of invitations, Kathy still cringed whenever she saw Kelly. Avoidance didn't work because Kelly would call her name loudly just as she tried to get away. Religious tracts appeared in her cell--before they made it into Kathy's wastebasket. Her friend even scheduled an appointment for her to meet with a Bible study leader. "C'mon, Kath. Will you just do it for me?"

Because of friendship and not faith, Kathy went. Shortly after this, a book describing a woman's vision of hell made her wonder, "What if what I'm reading is really is true?" Unable to put the book down, Kathy made her leap toward the other side of a canyon wider than most of us can comprehend. In the early hours of March 9, 1996, against the backdrop of an evil darkness and despair, Kathy landed on her feet safe on the Solid Rock!

Kathy was anxious to share her news. Her heart finally resonated with all of the "right words" she'd once spoken at His Mansion. Jailhouse religion had given way to the genuine article, and in April of 1998, Kathy invited everyone she could to her baptism. She wanted as many people there as possible--especially those who usually didn't come to church. One such woman, upon hearing Kathy's story, was moved to surrender her life to Christ.

Kathy, having landed on the other side, now calls others to follow her across the chasm created by sin.

They'll be other times when the fabric of Kathy's life will be torn, but she now has confidence that there are no canyons that cannot be safely vaulted. It has been my experience that there exist signs of hope and encouragement close at hand as we contemplate making the leap--provided we look for it.

IX. COMRADES ALONG THE WAY

The further you've traveled in your journey, the more welcomed are the well-wishers--veterans of life's adventures. Especially welcomed are those who line the trails edge cheering you on and offering words of encouragement. These newfound friends often have just what you lack, and occasionally, desperately need what you have to share. Cherish them; they are fellow pilgrims.

If you arrive in strange territory, one good place to find out what's going on is at the local "watering hole." I certainly wouldn't recommend this classroom as the best learning environment for most subjects, but I must admit that I gained valuable insight into community at a gathering of the clan where Irish stout issued from the draught like spring water from a rock. Everyone's toes were tapping to a lively fiddle tune and a strong sense of family prevailed.

Murphy's Pub had been the site of weekly Irish music sessions for years and on this particular evening twenty or so musicians assemble in circles and play hammered dulcimers, button boxes, bodhrans, fiddles, bouzouki, banjos, guitars, penny-whistles, flutes--even uilliean pipes. Celtic sounds from Ireland, Scotland, Cape Breton, Quebec, and Newfoundland found expression in jigs, reels, and strathspeys. Surely now, 'tis the music of heaven!

What intrigued me when I began to attend these sessions were the three concentric circles of chairs in which performers and participants sat. I had the sense that certain rules were in force that had neither been written nor dictated by any single individual. The inner circle of chairs held the dominant musicians of the session, while additional musicians and instruments populated the second. A third row held active spectators who may or may not have had their instrument tucked beneath their seats. The seating order had roots much older than any of the participants.

The music was lively, and inspired clapping, singing, and foot-stomping. How the musicians withstood the pace of end-to-end jigs and reels was beyond me. Less than half an hour into the session, one or two fellows rose to visit the facilities or to slake their thirst. As they stepped out of the circle, they would tap a musician in the second row who played the same instrument, and point to the now vacant chair, "Lad, you'll be sittin' in for me, huh?"

144

The young man or woman--nervous, but thrilled--took his or her place and someone else called out the next tune. This process was repeated throughout the evening. Soon the recently seated musician heard the inevitable. "Well lad, you'll be callin' the tune." The apprentice, who had been preparing for this eventuality since forever, stammered and then carried off the tune!

When the holder of the inner circle seat returned, the novice returned to his chair in the second row to await a future calling. Over the months I noticed that occasionally a seasoned musician did not return--off to seek new venues, I supposed. The veterans would invite the second-benchers whom they had come to respect to take a place in the inner circle--and so it went.

I started as a spectator in the third row, but was soon encouraged by others who sensed my enthusiasm to consider an instrument and get involved. I purchased a bodhran (an Irish hand drum) only to learn that only the accordion rivals its popularity in the hands of a novice! I finally settled upon the guitar. My guitar and I soon became a regular in the second row. One day I'll feel the tap. Only regular practice and participation will ensure that I'm ready!

*   *   *

Much like musicians in a session, fellow travelers can be a blessing, especially when you are all headed in the same direction. But if you have distinctly different agendas, staying together too long will be unproductive. Trying to walk together while disagreeing on major issues will only increase the weight you carry and create discord and disharmony. When folks who do not share your vision join you, they tend to play while you pay! It can be fun to join in and appreciate the camaraderie, but everyone's energy is required in order to reach a worthwhile goal. Having folks drop in and drop out, robs the community of valuable energy. I learned this lesson as I've learned most--the hard way!

*   *   *

In the spring of 1975 Graham Pulkingham, founder of a now defunct Christian community in Texas, was speaking at an Episcopal Church in nearby Greenwich, Rhode Island. Friends who had recently visited the oldest Christian community in the country (Bruder Hof in Norfolk, Connecticut) urged us to go with them to hear him speak. Pulkingham's vision for Christ-centered community kindled a flame that burned brightly in me and instilled a vision that would influence the remainder of my life.

No sooner had I begun "daydreaming" about community than a unique property with four apartments and eight secluded acres were brought to Joan's and my attention. We were not actually looking for property and would not have been able to afford anyway--not even a garage. But the owner, a rather eccentric Christian lady, had decided to move to Nova Scotia and felt "led" to make it possible for the Farmers to own her mini-estate. When opportunity knocks, run to answer the door! I was eager and excited. I couldn't pass it up. "The Hiding Place" would be the name of our new community. And all this was running concurrent with His Mansion!

Fulfilling this dream came with a price. Not only did I have the responsibility for a growing ministry, which competed with my marriage, but now three couples had essentially moved in with us! The couples were folks who had served at the Mansion and were now employed locally. They joined us on the property soon after Joan and I had settled in, leaving us little time to develop a sense of privacy and family cohesion. We had been married for fourteen years and looked forward to having our own home again. The provision of this home was an answer to prayer, but my tendency to turn *everything* into a ministry sabotaged it.

Living in close community leaves each member more exposed than does life in open society. There were times when we witnessed more than we cared to! On the other hand, there were insights to be gleaned and valuable lessons that were learned. Fred and Betsy, one of the families making up our experiment in community, had been missionaries in Colombia, and would teach us much! I suppose Columbia was where Fred had acquired the notion that his wife should be his servant. He was helpless. She did everything for him and as a result, those in our community, plus the regulars at our Wednesday night Bible study, resented him. Fred's manner of treating his wife was the very antithesis of how God intends a man to treat his wife.

Betsy, Fred's faithful servant, had retreated through the door separating our apartment from theirs to retrieve her Bible. While she was out of sight, Fred hollered, "Betsy, get me another iced tea," to which came the instant reply, "Get up and get your own!" The entire Bible studies group, as if on cue, rose to applaud and cheer the beleaguered servant. Fred was devastated, but Betsy was amazed by what she heard come out of her mouth. Betsy wasn't the only one to become exasperated with this manipulator, however.

Saturdays were common workdays at the Hiding Place and on one weekend in early January the men of this fragile experiment were cutting cordwood and lugging it into the basement. The snow was deep, the temperature freezing, and Fred was whining as usual. Early in the effort Fearless Fred dropped a log on his foot and fell down, crying out in pain. My son, Shawn, and another man lifted him up and carried him into his warm apartment.

Faithful Betsy began untying his boot--"Oh, Oh, Oh..oouch! No, no, please be gentle!" Then the injured warrior ordered his television to be turned on. Much to Fred's pleasure--certainly not surprise--the Houston Oilers were in the playoffs. Fred hailed from Houston, Texas. Momentarily, the Oilers scored a touchdown and Ol' Fred bounded into the air, jumping up and down and yelling like a cheerleader. So much for his injured foot. Shawn took note.

Later that spring, we purchased an 8-HP Troy-built rototiller for our community garden. Everyone was assigned duties and a share in the harvest. It was Fred's turn to cultivate the garden. The 'tiller had two power drives: one for the wheels and the other for the tynes. High tech, Fred was not!

"Dad, come here!" Shawn's yell got my attention. "You will not believe this. I'm going out and rototill that slug into the ground!" Fred had found the lever that made the digging teeth rotate all right, but hadn't been able to figure out how to make the wheels turn. At this juncture Shawn looked out the window and witnessed Fred harnessing his obedient wife, Betsy, to the tiller with ropes and urging her on as she pulled the rototiller like a mule. Shawn didn't need any urging! I had to restrain him. After gathering our emotions we went out and rescued Fred's beast-of-burden.

An advantage of community living is that it does provide opportunities for correction and reproof and it didn't take the other members of the Hiding Place long to express their feelings to Fred. During the years following God was working on Fred's self-centeredness to the point where today he and Betsy serve as an overseas missionaries again.

This ongoing experiment in community taught us a truth that we would not have learned in another setting. We discovered there are some basic principles at work in ventures of this magnitude. *Someone* has to supply the property. *Someone* carries the financial responsibility. *Someone* must already possess the majority of "stuff" necessary to operate. *Someone* ends up as the "parent" of the operation. Unfortunately that someone is often one-and-the-same couple. At The Hiding Place, it was Stan and Joan! A year after the experiment began, the Hiding Place became an apartment house where everyone took care of their respective responsibilities. It worked better that way.

Community--Christian community--is a by-product, not a prime product. When people cooperate to accomplish a common, worthwhile goal, and are willing to put personal preferences and agendas aside in the process, they may catch a peek of true community. But don't look too hard, or it may vanish!

* * *

Great adventures, like great organizations, require order and boundaries. The risk, however, is that boundaries that actually hinder healthy exploration may be established. Rich discoveries are lost and before we realize it, the hedge grows so high that the only way to scale it is with the help of a friend. One veteran of His Mansion's community agrees.

Kate made a return visit to His Mansion. She had a purpose. She felt that she had surrendered a principle while serving there that should not be negotiable and had returned to redeem it. She had, in her opinion, lived and worked under rule of law and given short shrift to grace. Kate visited to symbolically take her stand for grace, the principle her life now depended on.

Kate had mentored several women and supervised many interns and she wanted to do it right. Years later, she admitted, "When I was at His Mansion, I didn't have a clue that Christianity was a relationship." As Kate explained, she came to believe her own worth hinged on her performance. Today she readily admits, "That's not the gospel at all." In fact, she wonders how God could have used her when she'd had it all so wrong.

A former student, who once had only obscenities to share with Kate, eventually had different feelings to share:

I'm sittin' here thinking about how you say that God didn't use you. You were very vulnerable. It was by your example that I understood certain things. Whether you know God used you in those times or not, He did.... God uses us even when we don't know.... A thought, an action, a look, a touch, I mean, you just don't know how many times God used you. And I'm not saying that you're perfect... but God uses us in spite of us, in spite of our sin, in spite of anything.

The wonder of wonders is that God uses us in spite of the fact we are like sheep. Sheep need community. Separate a sheep from its companions and it will refuse to eat and soon die. Yet, it requires a certain amount of grace to shepherd sheep when they are in community. They are just so—sheeplike!

* * *

Three quarters of the way through Handel's *Messiah*, the chorus erupts with the strong musical phrase "All we like sheep." "All we like sheep" is repeated again, and the strong musical phrase wakes up a sleeping husband or two in the crowd. But do the singers and listeners get the message? I'm not so sure. Even in churches where people understand and know the message of the oratorio, many still don't appear as if they've ever spent time with mutton in the making.

After a particularly ruthless ice storm, Frank stood at his window surveying the scene. As he looked out at the shiny glaze, he noticed our small herd of sheep. Not keen on the ice, they stood like figurines on top of the hill. Uncomfortable. Uncertain. Taking the lead, one started down the hill. After a couple of steps, legs of lamb were leading a somersault demonstration extraordinaire. The show ended only when the venturesome leader hit the snow fence at the bottom of the hill.

Frank chuckled. Lamb Chop, one of the more personable sheep, was stuck. To make matters worse, his buddy at the top of the hill decided to join him. "All we like sheep." In a rousing replication of the leader's performance, it, too, slid smack into the snow fence--and stayed there. "All we like sheep." True to sheep nature, the next followed. *"All we like sheep."* Then the next and the next until they all lay in a woolly pile at the bottom of the icy hill.

Each sheep took its turn at the feat as if trying out for the circus. Frank watched in disbelief. Stupid sheep! Couldn't they see?

You can't chase sheep. They're followers. So it is with people. As long as a trusted leader is in sight, it is permissible--even healthy--to enjoy a swath of latitude as we meander along the path of life. The bottom line is that we're pretty bullheaded. The folks we hang with at the watering hole may help us get our bearings and provide invaluable advice. But without competent leadership, we're apt to spend time trapped in a thicket.

*   *   *

The Woodstock Fair--not the Woodstock of the '60s fame, but Woodstock, Connecticut--is one of the premier annual county fairs in New England. Situated on a thin boundary between the fast-moving, affluent, culturally refined, bedroom communities, and the genuinely rural, general store, tobacco chewin' farm country of New England, the clientele at the Woodstock Fair is as colorful as it is diverse. It is primarily a 4-H fair with agricultural exhibits, which has helped enhance its reputation as a "wholesome" event. During the '70s, 25,000 people went through the fair over the Labor Day weekends.

Each year at the Woodstock fair, the family from His Mansion set up a small stage under a lean-to roof. Those who played an instrument were encouraged to give it their best. When a crowd (six or more was a crowd) stopped to listen to the music, I would break in and share my own journey of faith or take a whirl at "soapbox preaching." If I was tuckered out or saw an opportunity to push an aspiring preacher off the cliff, I would nudge him in front of the microphone and say, "You're on!" It was sink or swim.

One afternoon in the fall of '75, a very attractive woman, but who looked like she had a chip on her shoulder, stopped in front of the booth. She stood for an hour and the longer she stood, the brighter and more radiant her face became. Like a caterpillar in the pupa, Paulette was being transformed from the inside out. Before I got the chance to interact with her, she disappeared and returned with a really big man--I mean low to the ground and wide!

Her husband Ron was the vice-president and chief operator of a large well-drilling firm in Northeastern Connecticut. Well drillers are known to be hard drinking, no-nonsense, rowdy folks. He sure looked the part. But 250 pounds plus of skeptical hardheaded roustabout was no match for six struggling young men and women in love with Jesus. The awesome power and gentle spirit of Jesus would shatter this block of granite. Ron and Paulette have been an important part of the adventure from that day to this.

*   *   *

Usually comrades join us on the trek because they are going in the same direction as we are and are motivated to combine their efforts with ours. However, just because we are headed in the same direction doesn't mean we are the product of the same history. We would do well to learn to appreciate our differences and our unique contributions. Most people's strengths are fairly evident, but Chris turned out to be a sleeper!

The only way you could be sure Chris was alive was with a stethoscope--or at least it seemed so. During room routine in the morning, if you didn't prod him and keep an eye on him, he was back in the sack. When he was awake, he was in a haze; when he did move, it was slow

One day Chris was assigned to the woodlot crew, which meant he and his co-workers had to climb part way up the summit. When the crew stopped for a breather, Chris settled down beside the path in the shade, near a wild berry patch,

down beside the path in the shade, near a wild berry patch, and actually dozed off--with a granite rock for a pillow! The crew chief's greatest challenge in managing this tough crew was keeping Rip Van Winkle awake. The assignment fell to Paul. Paul and his crew were tasked with hauling trees away that had been felled and cut into logs by Dean, the woodlot foreman. Forgetting that his primary calling was keeping Chris from impromptu naps, Paul got intrigued by an anticipated "timber-r-r-r." He explains:

> Suddenly, I was hit hard from the side and went flying to the ground with someone on top of me. I felt angry and was ready to hit whoever it was when I heard an enormous, earth shaking thud behind me. It turns out that my commonly comatose charge had seen a tree that had become hung up and was falling backwards toward me. Like a shot, Chris burst through the trees and knocked me away as the sixteen-inch tree landed where I had been!

Nobody had ever seen Chris run before!

Chris's 40-ft. sprint gave new meaning to an old principle: "Don't be quick to judge what you see on the outside. God can use the most unlikely people for His purposes." I agree wholeheartedly, and the story of another veteran attests to it.

When William McIsaac, Sr. asked for the hand of his North Ireland sweetheart in the late 1800s, he was told, "Not with that 'Mc' before your name!" McIsaac became Isaac--from Irish to Jewish in one fell swoop. Much later and after four years at New York City College, their son, William, Jr. landed his first--and last--job. He went to work for The Dime Savings Bank and retired forty-two years later. Bill's life was not without tragedy, however. His wife, Mary, had developed Alzheimer and had to be placed in a care facility. She no longer

I met Bill at the small church that he attended in Long Island. Although Bill was 65, he was among the youngest members of that congregation. I arrived in Seacliff, Long Island, with a van full of young men and women from His Mansion who were fresh off the streets and still craving drugs and alcohol. Our presentation included a prostitute and two recently hospitalized mental patients. We put on a program of singing and testimonies that had been rehearsed en route. The unusual cadre of wounded healers shattered the ordinary routine of that tiny church. Our act was so far from polished and staged that it was actually refreshing. We sang spiritual praise songs and told stories of healing and hope.

Everyone was touched, but Bill was especially impacted. He sat in the audience, enthralled. Here was a man who played the violin and attended opera. If he'd ever danced, it would've been in a tux. Yet, he thoroughly enjoyed this evening of singing and public speaking that was far below his usual fare.

The refined, slight-of-build, banker moved toward the front of the church when the program ended. He looked very distinguished with his graying hair, sharply trimmed white mustache, and paintbrush goatee. The young folks thought he resembled "Col. Sanders" of Kentucky Fried Chicken fame.

"Stan, I don't know anything other than banking," he said, "but I want to be with young people. I don't want to end up in Florida playing shuffleboard, counting pills, and talking incessantly about my most recent meal. I'll hold wood while someone else splits it. Anything. Can I be a part of your adventure?"

"You bet, Mr. Isaac!" I said. I had recognized for some time that our small, youthful community needed a mature presence. We needed a grandfather figure, someone that was clearly out of reach as a substitute father. Grandparents can give and accept love with less risk of becoming the object of resentment and transferred responsibility. We needed the seasoning of a senior and God provided one. "Yes, you're just what we need!"

Bill had another responsibility to attend to before he felt free to join His Mansion. The call came months later. "My Mary has gone home. I'm alone. Is there still a place for me?" The Mansion family had their Grandpa and I, a special comrade.

For many years at His Mansion, Bill ran errands, provided taxi service, and picked up repair parts. Each day he made the mail run and did our banking. Every merchant, waitress, and public servant in the valley recognized and welcomed this dignified gentleman as he worked his way through a busy daily routine.

At that time, I was driving and flying all over the United States and abroad. When Joan could not accompany me, Bill was my faithful companion. He became a familiar figure in the churches that we visited. Bill volunteered the use of his Volvo as long as I agreed to serve as his chauffeur.

Each of us has our peculiarities and left to ourselves, most personal quirks go unnoticed. Bill and I spent a lot of time together, and believe me, we became painfully aware of each other's peculiarities! By our learning to laugh rather than grind our teeth, our friendship deepened.

I would often step out of the car to stretch when we had arrived in a church parking lot. Getting back into the car to gather up my Bible, I'd notice a strange, pungent odor. The first time it happened I supposed the odor came from the car's engine. Bill didn't act like he noticed it, so I asked if he smelled anything. That's when I was introduced to one of those Heloise tips. Somewhere in his travels, Bill learned that he could apply an instant shoeshine by spraying WD40 on his shoes!

There were other oddities that I discovered during my travels with Bill. One was shuffling into the motel bathroom early in the morning to confront Bill's false teeth in the only available water glass--the other being half full at his bedside. Of course, there might have been some things about me that Bill found difficult to accommodate. After stopping for lunch, I would often express my satisfaction, or dissatisfaction, by expelling a loud burp, to which Bill would repeat his mantra, "Better a vacant house than an unruly tenant!"

For Bill Isaac, life, in many respects, began at age 65. Seldom had the young people at His Mansion seen such enthusiasm and satisfaction in a senior citizen, "establishment" type. They couldn't get enough of him and members of his office "harem" knew the way to his heart. Penny was one, among many in the office, who had Bill's special attention.

"Bill, can I drive? Please? Can I, can I?" Penny pleaded with her aging buddy. His eyes were failing, and riding with him could produce premature graying. She couldn't bear to tell him this, so she persisted with her pleading. "Please, Bill? Can I?" Swayed by her childlike enthusiasm, Bill handed over the keys.

In the earlier days, when his vision was sharper and he did the mail run solo, he'd stop twice at the grocery store. On the first visit, a pack of Fresca was placed in the store cooler. After stops at the post office and bank, he'd return for the chilled six pack, his gift to the office staff. These women were more than willing to call Bill their hero.

Bill served with that kind of enthusiasm until his health failed. When he was 83, my faithful comrade took off on a far more exciting trip with the only Friend he loved more than me. Bill's remains are buried in the cemetery on the backside of our hill.

*　　*　　*

The only individual in a typical family hierarchy, who could match Bill's status as the "resident Gramp," would be a grandmother. When "Grandma Jean" made her debut, there was no rivalry. Together Bill and Jean delighted the Mansion family and each other.

156

Ironically, Jean's faithful friend and husband had also developed Alzheimer's years before. Jean served him and cared for him as he became more of a youthful charge than a husband. Then Jean was alone. She lived with her daughter and son-in-law, Linda and Karl, until they launched out on their personal journey joining the His Mansion community. Because they took some of Jean's grandchildren with them, Jean decided to join them. His Mansion had a Grandma to complement Bill.

Being a retired schoolteacher, Jean volunteered to conduct the GED program, a high school equivalency certificate course. Many of the men and women who come into the His Mansion community seeking healing have not completed high school, but are certainly bright enough to do so. It was an amazing sight to see Jean, a gray-haired senior citizen making putty out of seasoned ex-cons like Carl Cartwright!

After her retirement, Jean occupied her considerable energies collecting and studying English Ironstone. Today, her books on the subject are considered the collector's bible. It didn't take long for this lady who spent her life touching, painting, and writing about cold, brittle vessels of English Ironstone to become a master at refinishing vessels of flesh. Under her gentle loving hand, some of the hardest were fashioned into valuable vessels of healing to others.

* * *

Before Bill and Jean's arrival, the His Mansion community had known only the occasional touch of an older hand, Gladys and Harold Griggs being among the most memorable. These and other veterans of life have taught me much. It makes sense for the teacher to be older. Yet surprisingly, some of the most refreshing regulars are underage:

Dear Mr. Farmer,

We pray for you on Saturdays. How much does a cow cost? We are praying about buying one for you. Our cow fund now has $37.50 in it.

157

Please let us know how much more we need to save, so we can send it all at once.

        Sincerely, Danny Gullege

It turns out that Danny was also writing on behalf of his siblings. The six, seven, and eight-year old children tithed their allowances and spent Saturday mornings not only praying for us, but doing odd jobs for neighbors in order to raise enough money to buy a cow. By unanimous vote of the Gullege children, our bovine baby was named before we picked her up at Agway. "Joy the Cow." That alone would have made her a standout among Stu Beef, and Sir Loin, but in addition to that the community also knew her history.

The Gulledge's gift did not end with the purchase of "Joy." The fifty dollars used to purchase Joy arrived in a January 9, 1998 letter which asked (among other things), *"How much does it cost to feed a cow each mounth[sic]?"*

*   *   *

Not every provision is a handout. Early one morning a '63 Dodge van filled with sleeping bags and boxes towing a shaky, red trailer and a Buick station wagon pulled out of the driveway of the original His Mansion in Wauregan, Connecticut, destined for truck-farms in Maine. We looked like a caravan of gypsies. We were headed to Maine to glean vegetables from harvested fields so we could preserve the food to help us survive the winter months.

Upon arrival, the grassy field in front of the small farmstead where my parents lived was transformed into a mini refugee camp. For about a week the tents, clotheslines, and makeshift potties added interest to the landscape that became our temporary home.

Several local farmers had finished harvesting and allowed us to enter their fields early in the morning to pick carrots, cukes, squash, beets, onions, and potatoes--anything that was left after the commercial harvesting. It seemed that potatoes were the most needed and most difficult to find. Our need was not unnoticed; God would provide.

On Cape Elizabeth (where buying a postage stamp-sized piece of property could put one in debt for life) the Maxwell family owned and operated a farm known throughout New England for its strawberries. Most folks appreciate the Maxwells' berries, but it was the spuds that attracted us.

In exchange for picking stones out of his fields, Ken Maxwell allowed us to load all the potatoes and other vegetables that the trailer could lug. Leftovers from their fertile gardens provided food to keep us alive and healthy for another season.

Today, more than twenty-five years later, Ken Maxwell and his sons continue to delight our community by giving us the privilege of picking fresh strawberries and filling our root cellars with hearty Maine potatoes. To put the icing on the cake, so to speak, Mrs. Maxwell prepares an all-you-can-eat lobster and corn-on-the-cob feast for our "poor, overworked pickers." What a benefit package!

* * *

Living in community and moving through life in a compact little troupe can result in becoming insulated from the world around us to an unhealthy degree. There's a tendency to develop a myopic view of the world and be content to huddle together. It can be frightening to expose ourselves and become vulnerable, but like my blind lady-friend taught me during our boat trips to off the island, the potential for discovery is worth the risks. The most exciting dramas of life cannot be seen from inside the holy huddle, a lesson I learned while sitting on a seaside bluff watching the tide come in.

Along the shore of my island home great tides would pull the ocean away from shore, leaving the landmass nearly twenty percent larger than it was at high tide. This process took place over a span of several hours and would leave tidal pools isolated among the rock ledges. Every pool becomes a world of its own for a few hours.

I discovered that when the ocean receded, the members of these small communities seldom strayed far from their pools. The bluish lobster would be in the hole under the quartz-laden stone. The large, green crab with the deformed claw would crouch beneath the same overhang of rock and seaweed near the mouth of the pool. A dozen "Gillies" would play endless games of hide-and-seek among the shells and stone.

The more I reflect on the individual pools I studied as a child, the more they remind me of *Cheers.* Even fish seem to want to be "where everybody knows your name!" Each pool appeared to be a distinct, separate world, that is, until the tide came in exposing it to the larger oceanside community. Our world can change quickly, introducing a new, sometimes unfamiliar system of hierarchy, threats, and opportunities. So it has been in my life.

My journey to the hill where I now stand has in many ways brought me full circle. In the security of my little pool, I am more appreciative of those whose journey has taken them in a slightly different direction in their quest to follow Christ. From a higher vantage point, it becomes clearer that we're all in it together. Let the tide come in!

X. A LITTLE "R&R"

Life moves so very fast. In an effort to get from one place to another--job to job--crisis to crisis, it's easy to stumble over the treasures and look right past the beauty. It's important to bivouac at day's end and light the campfire. It is in such moments of relaxation that the difficulties of the day are sifted and transformed into laughter and wisdom. Sharing stories, contributing your personal collection of gems, and encouraging one another will rejuvenate and recharge your batteries.

I've learned much about myself as I've reflected on some key events in life. One such event will not make the front page of the National Rifle Association's monthly magazine, although it did involve a firearm.

The bolt-action, single-shot, .22-caliber Stevens rifle was the most extravagant birthday present Dad had ever bought me and although it was used, I couldn't tell the difference. It was brand new to me.

Dad had given stern warnings about the dangers of guns and acquainted me with safe handling procedures. Under no circumstances was I to even *think* of aiming it at anything while in the house, even when unloaded. Practicing with real bullets would come later.

Sitting on my bed admiring this wonderful weapon, I was quite certain that it marked a passage from boyhood into the limbo that led toward manhood. Its solid wood stock, shiny blue barrel, and Rocky Mountain sights captivated me. I could hardly wait to load it, fire it, and clean it.

The small, cardboard brick of ammunition was kept in my dad's top drawer. I couldn't get over how heavy it seemed for such a compact, little block. As I slid the cardboard sleeve off the package and saw the checkerboard display of gray tips and bright brass caps, my heart began to race. I decided to hide them in my bedroom until I could inspect them without fear of being caught.

On Saturday mornings we were allowed to sleep in an extra hour, but on this Saturday I was awake at the break of dawn. The little box with the magnetic pull was beneath my pillow. Although it was only one inch square and two inches long, it had a power all its own. I couldn't resist. Again, I slid the sleeve from the box, only this time I poured the bullets onto the bedspread. Why the little missiles had such a dazzling effect on me I'll never know. Holding several of them in my hand, they seemed like nuggets of gold. As I jumbled them from palm to palm temptation began to sink her talons deep.

The bolt responded to my fingers like the fine piece of machinery it was. Cher-chunk. So sure--so reliable. *Stick the cartridge in the chamber and close the bolt. Reverse the process and the tiny jaw grips the edge of the cartridge and flips it out onto the bed.* It worked so perfectly. So slick. I couldn't wait.

Returning all fifty bullets to the box proved to be more difficult than pouring them out onto the covers. They needed to be replaced--one pointing down, one pointing up--to get them to fit. Finally they were in, not quite as tightly as before, but I supposed the box had loosened a little. I'd return them to Dad's bureau later that morning.

I turned my attention to my rifle once more. *Lift it, pull the shoulder pad tightly to my shoulder, balance the stock with my left arm, and sight along the shiny, blue steel barrel.* I put it down and repeated the action, quicker this time. Oh, I couldn't wait!

I knew Dad said it wasn't good to "dry fire" the weapon, but I'd done it before and the sharp click gave a satisfying substitute for the actual report of a bullet firing. So once more I pressed the butt against my shoulder and I lifted the stock up. I aligned the barrel and sights with the hole in the birdhouse in the back yard. Then I carefully squeezed the trigger. C-R-A-C-K!"

When I had recovered from the shock, I looked beyond the barrel to discover a tiny, perfectly round hole in the window. Amazingly, it was the same size as one of those cylindrical nuggets! Soon I had company in my bedroom. Lots of words filled the air, but I "heard" feelings that were much louder than words. My parents left the room and my wonderful gift left with them. I would not see it again that year.

Mourning my loss, I wandered out to the backyard. There was a fresh splinter of wood protruding from the rear of the birdhouse revealing a small exit-hole. There was no corresponding entry hole in the front. Bulls-eye!

Not all adventures end with our being able to laugh at ourselves while learning valuable lessons. Some lessons and examples are far too costly to produce amusement. We benefit greatly, however, when the mistakes and embarrassments that damage nothing but our own egos are converted into laughter. The miles will slip by faster when they are lubricated with mirth.

* * *

The famous chaplain, who sacrificed his life by surrendering his lifejacket to save a shipmate during W.W. II, was the son of another well-known Poling. His father, Dr. Daniel Poling, was once chairman of Christian Herald, the organization from which we purchased the mountainside in New Hampshire. The surviving Poling son settled on land abutting our community and when his parents passed away he had them interred in a private cemetery that is now part of His Mansion's property.

One moonlit night, shortly after taking possession of the mountainside village, I bundled up to the chill and struck out on a much needed walk to clear my head and to pray. A quarter of a mile up the wooded road, I came upon a brass plaque set in a huge, granite boulder. It read "Mother's Walk." I continued along the path.

The snow was bright and there was a full moon, so I was not particularly concerned about getting lost. I could see a small clearing at the end of the woods road, but kept my focus on the path in front of me to ensure safe footing. When I looked up as I approached the clearing, I nearly had a heart attack. There, twenty feet in front of me stood somebody's idea of Jesus--a white concrete statue created by one of the Poling sons in memory of his parents. I knew I would see Him some day, but I didn't expect Him to look exactly like the Sunday school stereotype but here He stood in the moonlight, shimmering white!

During my first winter on the mountain, I spent much of my time on site, getting things in shape to bring my family up from Connecticut. I stayed in a small room in the huge, unheated Long House. At night the building creaked and it was rumored that unseen entities roamed about freely. Who knows? I did hear some strange sounds.

Whenever possible my son Shawn accompanied me to New Hampshire and I made use of his strong back and limitless energy to dig a cellar beneath the "camp cottage" that we would one day call home. It gave us quality time together as well as a little "iron sharpening iron." One beautiful moonlit night, it occurred to me that the conditions were perfect for a visit to my concrete apparition. "Shawn, are you up for a walk?"--I told him I was going through a tough time and would value his input. That's all it took to motivate him. (Sometimes, I'm so devious it scares me!)

As we shuffled through the leaves, I began telling him about the rumors of ghosts in the Long House and the strange sounds that I had been hearing. He was getting a little jittery as we turned down a pathway into the woods that I knew as "Mother's Walk." Our gaze was directed toward the ground so we could make maximum use of the moonlight to guide our feet. As we entered the clearing, I stopped. "Do you hear that?" I whispered anxiously. Shawn's head rose quickly. Before him, less than twenty feet away, stood the shining white Jesus! Shawn must have jumped a foot off the ground. I've savored that delightful moment ever since!

Of course, Shawn did not keep that delightful experience to himself. Later that year, we held our first board meeting at the new facility. Shawn took Paulette Donovan, wife of one of the board members, down "Mother's Walk." On that clear, beautiful, fullmoon night, you could hear Paulette's scream for miles. She still loves Shawn, but he knows that one day he'll pay!

*   *   *

The New Hampshire hills are not the only place where the surroundings set the stage for laughter and amusement. His Mansion's pioneer effort on an isolated island in the Bahamas also provided some high times. A wealthy philanthropist owned a defunct scuba-diving resort on the remote island of Rum Cay and encouraged us to start a drug and alcohol rehabilitation center there. Because we had an initial phase program in Nassau, it seemed that a remote center might offer addicts a better chance of breaking free from the temptations in the city.

Rich and Laurie Strysko served as resident staff during the start-up of this missionary effort in "Paradise." Getting the rundown facility up and running as a healing community was the first order of business.

After a tiring day, the Stryskos retired to their tiny bedroom. About an hour after they had fallen asleep, Rich felt weight and movement on his knee. The full moon outside clearly illuminated the room and exposed their visitor. The Rum Cay Rodent--an overgrown water rat--stood on its hind feet, ten inches tall! Looking down from his regal pose, the rat found Rich and Laurie staring back at him and let out a challenging bark.

Rich bolted out of bed and donned a pair of welder's gloves that were on the dresser. The battle was on! Rich was wearing his gloves and, well, his gloves! The rat made a quick escape to the adjacent bathroom with Rich in hot pursuit.

Three looping left hooks failed to connect as the rat ricocheted off the walls, toilet, and floor, but the fourth sweep caught the critter squarely. The victor quickly wrung the rodent's neck. Had anyone been watching, they may have seen the gloved gladiator streak into the moonlit night and dispose of his victim. When Rich returned to the bathroom, he found his fair maiden well past the point of swooning over her champion; she was having a laughing fit! It was a welcome change.

Those who served in the healing community in New Hampshire were conditioned to find the humor in life wherever possible and the value of unscheduled comic relief. The Stryskos could recall when a young member of the community back in New Hampshire, where they had trained, provided such an occasion.

His name was Tommy O., and he was one of the youngest and most accident-prone guys to have been a part of our community. His hand repeatedly found itself between wood and other objects, even the log splitter. But his mangled, miracle hand wasn't his only trophy. While hiding under a truck during a game of capture-the-flag, a bee stung his foot. He jumped, whacked his head on the muffler, and was tagged by the opposing team. The guys liked their goofy little brother, accidents and all. Nowhere did his awkwardness evoke more laughter than when they played sports together.

"Next touchdown wins!"

The game was tied, and the sun was about to set. Sock flags hung from pockets and five-gallon mortar pails marked the sidelines--five on each side. The offense had thrown three incomplete passes and was on the last play of the game. Nobody expected what came next. Dave Spinelli offers a play-by-play:

"HIKE! Everyone goes long! The Quarterback drops back and lets the Hail Mary fly! All the wide receivers were in the end zone, but the ball was terribly under thrown, falling far short, right into a circle of the members of the opposing team. I watched the ball fly over my head, and, knowing it was short, my mind had already began celebrating victory. Suddenly, I was shocked by the most unimaginable sight. Nothing could've prepared me for what I saw. If you had told me what was going to happen before hand, there's no way I would've believed it.

"I saw Tommy O. catch the ball.

"It was a ridiculous, sloppy, contorted, off one thigh,

half slipping off the stiff fingers of his right hand, catch. But somehow he hung on. Don't ask me how. Recalling it now, still I can hardly believe it. But he caught the flippin' ball!

"I think everyone had the same reaction that I did. We stopped dead in our tracks, in shock. Except for Tommy. He started running.

"Only he started running the wrong way! Pandemonium broke loose. Between the bursts of laughter, the shouts from his teammates, and Tommy's own growling yell, Tommy's teammates were trying to grab him to turn him around.

"'You're going the wrong way!' I yelled. I tried to point him in the right direction. With his own team trying to push him toward the end zone, and the others grabbing for his socks, the clumsy receiver was tackled before he made a touchdown.

"Laughing, cheering, and yelling, guys from both teams hoisted the hero on their shoulders and carried him, ball in hand, into the right end zone!"

*   *   *

This "can-do, it's-okay-to-fail" attitude on the part of the His Mansion family also fosters in others the will and courage to keep trying. This was evident in another *ad hoc* football game that took place at His Mansion.

"You can make it in this sport," the roommates encouraged Nick. "This is you, man." Nick had the build, but understood "down" as a disposition, not a goal in a game. Nevertheless, his roommate prevailed, and Nick found himself playing a game he barely understood. Shortly into the game, Nick accidentally caught the ball. Dumbfounded, he cried out, "What do I do? What do I do?"

*   *   *

Whether by instinct or instruction, Nick ran. Nobody could catch him. Six points. The guys shook their heads and chalked this one up to beginner's luck.

But the beginner kept catching the ball. Testosterone levels escalated. It wasn't funny anymore! Still, no one tackled him. Despite his Greek heritage, the rookie experienced a little "luck-o-the-Irish" and his continued good fortune began to grate on his teammates. In his defense Nick sputtered, "I didn't mean to do this. What's going on? God, what are you doing to me? I'm just an innocent guy. The ball came to me, and I was asked to run with it."

* * *

As I watched Nick, his situation seemed vaguely familiar. I remember being just as befuddled as he when I intercepted the directorship of His Mansion. "It was my job to take it and run with it." From my perspective now, I realize how appropriate it is to thank the folks who pushed me.

Sometimes, a push is just what we need. At other times, we suffer the embarrassment of having our feet fly out from under us. When it's evident that we can stumble, yet get up and laugh, we're encouraged to continue on.

The view from my office window is always delightful and the scenery is breathtaking, but it's the people who provide the show. This is especially true during the winter months on the hill. Admittedly, my enjoyment is at another's expense. I have observed that after losing control of both feet and settling on the ground, the fallen victim stands quickly and looks around to see if anyone saw the fall. If there are no observers present, some will advance cautiously, while the cocky ones invite an encore.

During one spectacular sleet storm, a receptionist whose office view differed only slightly from mine decided she could no longer keep the humor to herself. "That was a 10!" She proclaimed over the PA system after one set of legs and arms went in opposite directions. Suddenly every ice-walker's fears were confirmed: They were being watched! Worse, they were being rated! Yet, in that instant, the fear was transformed. With no one worse for the wear, the embarrassment was transformed into laughter.

Further down the hill, another event was getting underway. One guy, in the process of doing chores, came sliding out of the barn, lead rope in hand, with a calf sliding behind him. Halter and lead intact, the calf proceeded to slide down the steep grade on his side. Still clinging to the rope, the young man rode down the hill behind it on the seat of his pants. It was His Mansion's version of the Nantucket Sleigh Ride!

It is one thing for a rugged young man and a calf but quite another for a damsel six months pregnant. This could be no laughing matter. The scene took place on the road leading to New Beginnings, our program for pregnant women in crisis. It was with inadequate forethought that we placed this unique part of our community on the highest part of the campus. It is a struggle for pregnant women to climb the hill at the best of seasons, especially for those who are mid-to-late term. It can be outright scary making the climb during the winter months. A lone trekker was sighted in a crouched position facing the right direction, but rapidly losing thirty hard-earned yards.

It was one of those miserably cold mornings when the students who were grouped together on their hike to the dining room looked like a cadre of cigarette smokers out for a stroll. It was so slippery that the only way to safely transport a pregnant student to the day's activities was by sled. The pregnant girl's intern decided to tow her to breakfast. All went well until the tow-ee ran over the tow-er. The intern hadn't fully calculated the cost of her commitment. As she watched her pregnant charge zip down the hill ahead of her, she realized what they'd overlooked: "How would she stop?"

Getting started is the easy part. Knowing when, how, or where to stop is always challenging. Doing so with grace is a triumph. My secretary, Vivian, gave all of us a lesson in this kind of grace one Christmas--a good lesson for me to learn.

We were all busy indoors, creating what for some would be the first set of positive Christmas memories they'd ever had. Turkey or ham sure tastes better without the garnish of dad showing up drunk or a minor disagreement turning into W.W. III. Outside, however, the ice was building. Rain had been falling all afternoon, turning the forest into a giant crystal Christmas display. The trek to our individual homes or dormitories could be an adventure, but sand would be spread on the road before everyone left.

Vivian, 60 years young, and full of confidence, didn't wait to follow the crowd, or for the sand. She was ready to head home early, so she shuffled from the porch to the dirt road running through the center of the campus. Immediately she slipped on the ice and sat down. Every attempt to stand was conquered by the stuff beneath her feet. Ever the lady, however, Viv resigned herself, relaxed, and enjoyed the slide. This wouldn't have been her first choice in transportation, but it worked. Still, the question remained: "How would she stop?"

By this time, those who were milling about inside had turned their attention to the hill outside. Just as if it were planned, Vivian's ride slowed to a stop where the hill leveled off--right in front of her door. Unaware of her watching fans, she gracefully stood, brushed off the frost, and skated inside.

Thanks for the lesson, Viv. It's impossible to always predict where the footing is treacherous and fear may well overcome us while we are out of control. But the journey is much more pleasant if we handle the upsets with dignity and grace.

* * *

Even when events unfold that have all the hallmarks of a violent video game, do your best, be responsible, and laugh when you can! Events that developed in the barn while stripping bark from pine poles may serve as a great illustration. We had been given a stand of Norway Pine to cut and haul away. Norway pine makes excellent fence posts, but only after the bark has been removed and the wood treated to prevent rot. A drawknife is used for this task. The job must be done carefully because the razor-sharp blade is repeatedly drawn toward the belly of the person wielding the knife.

Al LaMorey was in charge of several young men who had been assigned to the detail. A summer intern from Dartmouth College had volunteered for the summer and was also numbered among the work detail. It was hoped that our Dartmouth scholar, Steve, might add a certain level of culture and refinement to the residents who were in recovery from various dysfunctions. Yeah, right!

One of the students on the detail had, in previous years, assailed his senses with immense amounts of psychotropic drugs, mainly "acid." On this particular day, he was in a state of anxious frustration. Without warning, he ran into a nearby pig stall, and with his drawknife, hacked a pig's back with the debarking tool, cutting the hog's back to the bone. It is a tribute to the protective hand of God that he did not attack a fellow worker.

An intern ushered the "mad hacker" off to the dorm to be calmed and counseled while Dr. Dartmouth, Al Lamorey, and several students were left to deal with the injured pig. The emotional intensity was exacerbated by the pig's horrendous shrieks. The gash was six inches long and an inch deep suggesting that the animal would certainly have to be "put down." But Dr. Dartmouth courageously embarked upon an effort to save the pig. Someone ran off and returned with gauze, tape, a bottle of iodine, a huge needle designed for sewing leather, and fishing line monofilament for thread. The Chief Physician of the Bovine Rescue Team emerged from the canning room wearing a white apron and positioned himself on the rail of the hog pen to direct the operation. There, he whipped out a pocket cassette recorder and commenced narrating the procedure as if the crew were medical students working in a teaching theater. He began:

"Today we have Dr. LaMorey, famous surgeon from the renowned Mary Hitchcock Medical Hospital. The incision has been sterilized and..."

The hog squealed so loudly that it hurt onlookers' ears. The narrative continued but was interrupted by a series of pain-filled squeals each time the needle was stabbed into the pig's back.

With the operation finally over, a heavy belt of iodine-soaked gauze was wrapped around the pig and she was isolated in a clean pen. Anyone with an ounce of veterinary knowledge wouldn't have given her one chance in a hundred of survival. But survive she did, growing to a size that qualified her for a quicker, less painful end. Bacon!

I was elsewhere during this fiasco and the subsequent medical theater dramatization. Had I been present, I would have had the pig slaughtered, but I knew nothing about it until a week later when I was beginning yet another extended public relations trip. As I was getting into my car, "Dr. Dartmouth" handed me a cassette which I assumed to be a sermon, telling me he had been "really blessed" by it. He encouraged me to listen to it as I traveled, so I took it with me.

Typically I use the first fifteen minutes of a long trip to get adjusted--heat, seat position, and windows. After settling in, I often put a tape in the player and hope time passes quickly. If my young college friend had been blessed, perhaps I would be as well. I popped the tape into the player and within five minutes I was laughing so hard I had to pull off the road. Even after I started driving again, it was difficult to see through my tears.

I'd like you to think that all the awkward situations that have provided valuable lessons came at someone else's expense. But I've provided my share, and not always with the poised grace that Vivian demonstrated. My embarrassments usually happen when I rush along too fast and lose my footing. But rather than fall gracefully, I fight to maintain my balance--only to end up in a heap on the ground with a foot in my mouth.

Be prepared to learn from these "falls," because often that is why they happen. It is pointless to try to convince everyone around you that it was all planned and merely a part of your "routine!" It is also wise to slow your pace. Usually in my case that means stopping to think things through before my quick tongue leads me to perilous new heights (or lows).

*   *   *

On one occasion, I was invited to explain the function and importance of His Mansion to a large assembly of senior citizens gathered in a New Jersey church. The charge was to speak about drugs and I was going to give them an education they'd not soon forget. I was successful in that, I can assure you!

For the first fifteen minutes, I regaled them with horror stories of drug-induced schizophrenia and violence. I explained how addiction leads to suicide, prostitution, and fatal diseases. Kleenex came out of purses and the cuffs of blouses, as I told stories of family tragedies, shattered lives, and babies born into addiction. Oh, yes, I had them spellbound.

Wanting to share a recent bit of insider medical info, I proceeded to explain how cocaine is ingested. "Currency, often hundred dollar bills, are rolled up to form tubes or straws, and then inserted into one nostril, while a finger obstructs the other. Carefully formed lines of snow-white powder are then pulled--snorted-- through the money-straw into the nose." I went on to tell how the chemical is carried by the blood, from the lungs, and directly to the user's brain. They were with me. I had 'em. But I didn't know when to stop.

Deciding to really impress them, I proceeded with a colorful ad lib, informing them that, "snorting cocaine this way causes the crystaline powder to impinge on the membrane in the nose that divides on side from the other.   This, in time, I informed them, can result "in a deviated scrotum."

Within nanoseconds my mind was screaming, *Septum! Septum! You nut!*

My body temperature rose like a rocket. I steeled myself, mentally clothing myself with the garment of denial, and proceeded through the lecture as if I had not said or heard anything so outrageous. My resolve was sorely tested when I spotted a red-faced gent gagging as he tried unsuccessfully to stifle his laughter. More than one delicate elbow was launched into the side of an about-to-erupt husband.

As people exited the church, one woman rushed right on by me, staring straight ahead, but her mate, a grisly old goat barely able to contain himself, grabbed my hand, and complemented me on the most stimulating talk he'd ever heard in that church!

A central lesson to be learned from these illustrations is that seldom are things so serious in life that we cannot afford to laugh at ourselves while providing others the opportunity to laugh with us.

XI. COMMITMENT TO THE UPHILL CLIMB

Joan and I were headed for the glacier fields in the Canadian Rockies when we came upon switchbacks etched into the side of a great mountain. They had been carved by sheep, goats, elk, and people who had traveled this route long before we arrived. Our trip was slowed considerably by the need to reverse direction and sometimes even tthe need to climb downward for a distance before resuming the upward climb. While switchbacks made the climb possible, they also tested our commitment to reach the top.

Back in 1971 when we began this amazing experiment, word of a place where the hopeless and hapless could find refuge spread fast. Soon the bedrooms were filled and we were turning people away. A skeleton crew of zealous, but inexperienced staff could hardly be expected to provide for the security needed for fragile residents. Until somebody older became available who could take over and relieve me, allowing me to return to secular employment, the Mansion was my home away from home four nights a week. This temporary assignment has stretched on for thirty years!

I remember sailing into the main harbor at Guam, amidst the pomp and ceremony of a full military band while atop a brand new nuclear powered submarine. Seeing me dressed in my best formal whites, it would be impossible to know that all this came only after three days of wiping oil, shining brass, and scooping spit and cigarette butts from filthy bilges. It's the "iceberg" story all over again: for everything that is visible, there is much more beneath the surface. Significant, meaningful achievement, usually involves strain, pain, and no little discomfort. I was again earning my stripes in the trenches.

To be saddled with the title of "older person" is pretty sad when you're only 30 years old. I was certainly already too old for this routine! Nevertheless, I bedded down in a sleeping bag on the couch in the office so I could keep an eye on the main entrance.

*   *   *

Someone entering the house was not as great a concern to me as the possibility of trouble from an internal wanderer. At this particular time, we were dealing with the mystery of the "Phantom Crapper." Every three days or so, over the course of several weeks, someone discovered a new deposit. The culprit was sneaking out of his or her room at night and defecating in a new location each time. Halfway up the staircase, in the mudroom, in the laundry room—anywhere but the bathroom!

Tonight I was ready. I bedded down in my sleeping bag but I was fully clothed and armed with a three-cell flashlight. But as the single hours arrived, my eyelids grew heavy and finally, dreaming that I was fully awake and alert, I conked out.

Someone is watching me; I just feel it. The sensation, or awareness, became clearer as I mentally shook loose the cobwebs. *Nah!* My mind fought back. *Oh, yeah!* My sense persisted. I could feel it. Someone was watching me. Adrenaline began to course through my system. I awoke, and cracked an eye open ever so slightly, while clicking on the flashlight hidden deep in my sleeping bag. Slowly I eased the light up with a palm cupped over the lens. As my hand slipped away, the beam struck the floor right next to the couch. The spotlight focused on a pair of big ugly feet. Moving the light upward revealed a pair of hairy legs. Higher...oh, this was too much!

Mack was a very troubled young man who had tripped on powerful acid until his mind short-circuited. I had met Mack while visiting the Norwich State Hospital, a facility for the mentally ill. In any case, Mack was the prime suspect. "Get to your room right now, before I bend this flashlight around your head," I shouted. To accelerate his forward progress, I rapped each step behind him with my light-sabre. "Get! Get! Get!"

My thumping, banging, and yelling awakened other residents. Back in his room, I interrogated Mack, but the inquiry was interrupted by the shriek of a terrified female. One of the women had stumbled, barefooted, upon the latest smelly offering that had been left right outside her door!

Matt confessed to being the culprit and the mystery was solved. He was issued a penalty commensurate with the crime but refused to comply, and left the following day. When I raised my hand, pledged allegiance, and said, "I do" to Uncle Sam, I didn't receive a contract or union book with a list of rights and privileges. I received a list of duties and responsibilities. Similarly, commitment at the deepest levels doesn't come with terms, conditions, and escape clauses, but the heroic young men and women who had signed up to serve at His Mansion hadn't envisioned messy jobs like this one!

As we pursue the goal, two prime factors test our resolve and challenge our commitment. One is frustration, as in the above story. The second is fear.

* * *

One young woman was very troubled and had made several suicide attempts while at His Mansion. A touch of schizophrenia and a sizable dose of paranoia went a long way toward explaining the missing kitchen knives that had been found beneath her mattress. Any planned attempt to follow through on some bizarre escapade had been foiled, but where there's a will, there's a way.

All the buildings at the Mansion have the option of being heated with wood or oil. Using wood provides valuable work opportunities and saves money. The need for regular attention while burning this fuel creates an unusual problem, however. Someone must travel from building to building throughout the night ensuring that the fires don't go out.

Those who agree to join us in this community of healing seldom consider their contract as a life-or-death commitment and surely, Tom never thought of it in this light. He was, after all, only the "night stoker." Wandering around the grounds in the dead of night can be a scary proposition, but performing this task in a place where various members of the community suffer from emotional disorders adds to the apprehension.

In several buildings the furnaces are located in sheds adjacent to the main structure. The furnace stoker visits each of these sheds every few hours during the night. Tom, a quiet introspective sort by nature, entered the shed attached to the women's dorm and immediately sensed a "presence." Suddenly, out of the shadows emerged a nightgown clad figure wielding a hay sickle.

Fearing that he had intercepted the Grim Reaper making rounds, Tom retreated to his quarters. No matter who it turned out to be, this ended Tom's stoking career. The stalker in the furnace room experienced healing from her emotional condition and later laughed at the incident. Today, even Tom laughs about it.

*　*　*

In addition to battling the "demons" of frustration and fear, anyone who pursues any worthwhile endeavor can expect opposition. Certainly I have suffered the effects of that evil saboteur who delights in planting land mines in the path of our greatest and best intentions. As a young man, I wrestled with life-dominating, destructive habits and made sincere, heartfelt commitments to change--only to experience the agony of defeat again and again! Later in life I discovered that had I held on just a little longer at the height of my temptation, the enemy would have become discouraged and departed in search of another victim. Victory is often just over the hill. The enemy may win a skirmish from time-to-time, but the battle will ultimately be won if we persevere. Our attempt to establish the healing community on Rum Cay, one of the southernmost islands of the Bahamas, is an example of this.

Of the four original settlements on Rum Cay, only Port Nelson, population 45, remains. Salt for preserving codfish in the holds of sailing ships bound from New England to Europe was once the island's chief export. Electric refrigeration gradually replaced salt as the method of choice in preserving food. Growing pineapples for the American and British markets replaced salt as the island's chief export, until a monster hurricane in the eighteen hundreds swept seawater over the island, killing off the pineapple crop and permanently altering the soil. When the His Mansion staff arrived in Port Nelson to begin this outpost, there were no public utilities, no public water supply, no paved roads, no cars, and no tourists.

Yes, I know! The dismal prospect of suffering for God on sandy beaches, cool drinks in hand and ocean lagoons beckoning. Ha! Although some may not have believed this was the mission field, indeed it was. Our goal for this remote island community was to duplicate the dynamics of our New Hampshire community and provide a haven for dysfunctional addicts who were trapped in the crime and drug ridden city of Nassau. It sounded like a great plan at the time.

For Carl Cartwright, it *was* paradise. He had been raised on the "family island" of Long Island in the Bahamas, fifteen miles west of Rum Cay. He, of all people, should have known better! Food and mail came once a week by mail boat--a two-day cruise from Nassau. The island's telecommunications system consisted of one phone booth operational for only one hour each day. Carl's wife, Debbie, a mom with a three-month old infant, discovered that the nearest doctor was in Nassau--a four-day round trip on the mail boat. Making sure the Cartwrights were aware of how they felt about them, the island welcoming committee proceeded to give Debbie the silent treatment. She was white and she was not Bahamian! Paradise? Debbie would disagree.

Given their isolation, the Cartwrights and their colleagues welcomed any visitors from "off island," and subconsciously, most nonresident natives of the island rarely looked toward the sea without scanning the horizon for potential visitors.

The white sails were spotted long before the hull came into view. The yacht was indeed bound for Rum Cay, a favorite stop en route from the Caribbean to Nassau. *The Bahamas Cruising Guide* advertised the island as having "ice, food, and water available during daylight hours," and believe-it-or-not, with a meager population of 45, it boasted a restaurant and bar! Rum Cay is also known to be the second landfall of Columbus in the Americas.

Carl was the first to spot the sails and the excitement grew as the yacht continued its approach toward Rum Cay. As there was little fuel available for powerboats, sailboats had this idyllic port to themselves.

The sleek 36-footer anchored just inside the reef. The couple who rowed the tender ashore proved to be avid conversationalists, but the one crewman who remained aboard was not interested in small talk. He was dead! Fighting the stench on the boat, three His Mansion staff members worked to get the body out of his bunk and ashore.

An island resident who had been to nursing school in Nassau declared the silent guest officially dead and the first bit of business should have been a burial. But never let it be said that rigor mortis and odor can stand in the way of Bahamian bureaucracy! I suspect her decision to order an autopsy had more to do with the promise of a free trip to see her relatives in Nassau as "guardian of the cadaver," than of any real concern regarding the cause of their visitor's demise.

The mail boat was not due to arrive for a few days, so the "dearly departed," decaying guest needed suitable quarters. Wrapped in a plastic sheet and strapped to a stretcher, he was placed standing in the island's only walk-in cooler--ours! No one would be raiding the refrigerator while he stood guard! For weeks following, the cooks looked as if they expected him to greet them when they opened that door.

*   *   *

Things were heating up between the His Mansion folks and the locals. Several Bahamian women had their eyes on Mr. Carl and were jealous of Debbie.
They circulated rumors intended to divide the interracial

183

couple. The criticism was contagious and stress arose even between members of the missionary team. Something sinister was at work.

Now three things are common to Rum Cay: land crabs, cockroaches, and voodoo--and they are sometimes related. Deb opened her door one morning to discover a dead crab with its legs carefully rearranged. It was a message, and Deb was frightened, but comforted by the fact that Carl was expected back from New Hampshire in a few days. The following day she arose to find a similar arrangement of cockroach legs and wings on her dining counter. There were no bodies, just appendages. She was the object of someone's curse and she knew it. Not only that, but the perpetrator had been inside her apartment. She could hardly wait to relay the events to Carl and have him address it.

To Deb's disappointment, her husband merely placed their child's tricycle and toys around the entryway to startle nighttime intruders. Carl was a native. He knew all too well about voodoo, but believed that his new source of power and strength was stronger. God would be his protector.

The Cartwrights were protected, but the water storage cistern became the alternative target. Sabotage followed the voodoo. Fresh water is the lifeblood of the islands and His Mansion supplied everyone on the island with water from a huge cistern kept full by reverse osmosis machines that we had purchased and installed. The building that housed the $15,000 water maker was set on fire--the first strike. Tears came from more than just smoke. Someone had smashed the four-inch PVC pipe from the cistern, sending 50,000 gallons of fresh water rushing into the Caribbean. Talk about cutting off one's nose to spite their face!

Yet, in their efforts to establish a healing community in Rum Cay, Carl and Deb went beyond wishing, to believing, and beyond believing, to action. Their efforts at gardening illustrated the level of commitment and heart attitude needed to persevere on the uphill climb.

The smaller Bahamian islands are comprised of a sprinkling of dirt on a pile of dead coral. The few places where soil has accumulated hosts a tangle of thicket and jungle. The mere mention of planting a garden elicited, "Mon, ya can't grow nuttin' in dis place!" Only the heart of a born farmer would disagree with the local wisdom. Carl has that heart. Composting leaves, busting up coral, and lugging soil from remote caches finally yielded a garden that became a local attraction. The ministry itself, however, was less appreciated. An opportunistic American who owned land on Rum Cay seduced the already agitated locals with the promise that if they agreed to pressure His Mansion to depart, rich Germans were prepared to purchase the compound, establish a resort, and provide high paying jobs for everyone.

Rather than divide the families living on Rum Cay, and worn down by petty bureaucratic harassment, we took the non-binding vote of the natives as our cue. We pulled up stakes and planted a new work in the Canadian Maritimes, where we were welcome.

The rich Germans never did come to the islanders' rescue. The resort was never built. The greedy entrepreneur went bust and a hurricane flattened all the buildings on the compound the following year!

This account reads like something less than victory. What lessons were learned? The facility was ideal and the location "exotic." Great wealth was pledged to underwrite the project. But money, materials, and magic won't make for success and not every pioneering effort is guaranteed to be successful no matter how much we desire it to be.

God is ultimately more interested in how we behave in the process than the appearance of success. Everyone who was a part of this valiant effort has gone on to raise healthy families, continue in rescue work, or become assets to their communities. They have all seen first hand, that to really enjoy victory one has to understand and persevere through defeat.

185

We do welcome the times, however, when God shows up to rescue us and turn a very uncomfortable and inconvenient situation around. We crave immediate victory, but this isn't always the way God works. More often than not, He helps us to endure trials and equips us to press on to victory. Donna exemplifies this truth.

*   *   *

There was no question that life would be a difficult uphill climb for Donna. I met her at the door of my sister's home in Maine. Her speech was badly slurred. She had uncooperative facial muscles and walked only with great difficulty. Despite the fact that she had been born with cerebral palsy, Donna was attractive, but I had difficulty looking her in the eyes, nonetheless. I suffered from a genetic form of Irish guilt--the old "why her and not me?" syndrome.

When Donna heard about the exciting venture in which I was involved, her face broke into a radiant emanation of joy that took me completely off guard. She was working toward a degree in rehabilitation at the University of Maine and needed a practicum. Would I consider allowing her to do it at His Mansion?

"Da, er, umna, uh! Well—well...I, I guess so! (Translation: "What have I gotten myself into?") Soon my stammering acceptance became a reality. Donna McIntyre joined the staff as an intern. She moved into one of the two overfilled rooms of girls and began what was intended to be her practical training. Time would show that it would be everyone else who would learn invaluable lessons from her.

Although she was severely handicapped, she insisted on being treated the same as everyone else. The workload was tough and the ordeal of going up and down three flights of stairs several times a day was nearly impossible. For Donna, just communicating with others all day would be more work than the rest of us had to perform. Yet she smiled, gritted her teeth, and persevered.

186

Each morning, Donna trudged out to the garden on legs that seemed to have minds of their own and that might give way under her at random. The hot garden work caused her to perspire and being unable to fully control her facial muscles, she would also drool. As the mosquitoes singled her out, she swatted at them but her random swipes only smeared dirt across her face. By lunchtime she would have garden dirt up her nose and in her ears, eyes, and hair. When the lunch bell rang, Donna was often unable to stand. Frequently, she entered the house by crawling up the front stairs on her hands and knees. All the while, Donna's signature smile beamed God's grace to the point that others drew energy from her.

One day after lunch Donna was assigned to clean windows in the attic. I went up to check on her and found her weeping bitterly. Never before had I seen her cry. She was discouraged and completely worn out by her attempts to keep up with every one else. Our "trouper" was ready to call it quits and return home. Her inspiring countenance had become far too valuable to others and me, to let her go. In a world of weakness and conniving, Donna was a vein of true moral strength and purity, yet she needed our understanding and compassion. When we modified her schedule to a half-day of labor, she was able to stay.

On Thursday evenings, an exciting social gathering and Bible study took place at His Mansion. It was open to visitors and a number of neighbors usually showed up. Mike Kennedy, then a student at Alstead College in New York, stopped by every week en route to his home in Maine to attend the gathering and to spend time with the young woman of his dreams.

Mike seldom missed a week. He was in love with Donna. Donna, however, was convinced she'd never marry. Just completing college would be a monumental achievement.

By summer's end, Donna had fallen so in love with her co-workers and the troubled members of our community that she suggested postponing going back to the university so she

187

could serve for the remainder of the year. That plan seemed ill-advised to me. I encouraged her to go straight back to school and finish lest she end up married, pregnant, and not able to continue.

My prediction was not far off. Our smiling Donna returned to the University of Maine in September, married Mike in January, and was pregnant by February. She completed her BS in rehabilitation in June at the University of Maine.

Years later, while Joan and I were hiking around the island of my youth, we spied a lady coming toward us with two kids in a carriage and two more children hanging on. All had ice cream cones in hand, including the mother. The children, being children, were covered with dripping, sticky ice cream. The mother, being Donna, was also covered with the dripping delight. Donna smiled at us in recognition and by the time the hugging was all over, Joan and I were also covered with the sticky cream.

Like Donna, Al LaMorey's climb was uphill from the start. Both of Al's parents were alcoholics and early life consisted of frequent moves and fragmenting family.

Sometimes the obstacles in our way as we ascend the slopes are of someone else's doing, while others are of our own fashioning. Al, although handicapped by his environment, had dumped his own rubbish in the road and then plowed into it. He had followed the music-led drug culture to Watkins Glen, California and every other drug-drenched "happening" he could thumb to; like a rat behind the Pied Piper. Arrests and one-night stays in drunk-tanks lay in his wake from coast to coast. Back in his hometown, Al was a familiar face to local law enforcement officers.

I first met Al near the footbridge behind Polaski's Bar where he was standing amidst broken bottles, empty cigarette packages, and used drug paraphernalia. Bubble gum matted his long stringy hair, his eyes had been blackened, and his nose had been broken. Al was so wasted at this point in his life, that he ingested various kinds of drugs indiscriminately and without regard for where they came from or what they might do. This reckless life-style resulted in a frame designed to carry 250 pounds weighing only 130 pounds! He was in no shape to listen to me even if he had been sober--which he was not.

Several days before my first encounter with Al, he had been initiated to the deadly sting of a syringe filled with heroin. It would turn out to be the one time he would ever "shoot up." He didn't get the opportunity to inject heroin again because the following morning he was apprehended.

Al was well known in Danielson as a local "druggie" and had alienated the local police. They handcuffed him and knocked him to the ground. Placing a foot on the chain between the cuffs, one officer kicked Al in the face, which accounted for his broken nose. The emaciated "druggie" resisted, and they returned the following day to arrest him for "assault on a police officer." The judge sentenced him to a year in the Brooklyn Correctional Center.

My second encounter with Al was through a weekly Bible study that I taught in the prison. Michael Mageau, whom I was mentoring to be my teaching replacement to lead the study, befriended Al. Al's diligence and consistency encouraged Michael, even though the inmate, more often than not, came to class stoned. Inevitably, the rough and tough lawbreaker softened. Michael shared with Al that God wanted to forgive him for everything he had done wrong and had sent His own Son, Jesus, to take the punishment for him. Al broke before God and became a follower of Jesus Christ.

In 1976, just four days after his release from jail, the new believer knocked on the door of His Mansion. He was so damaged from drug abuse that he literally could not put a full sentence together. Talking to him was like trying to hold a conversation with someone who was brain damaged. Gradually,

189

the cloud of confusion dissipated as the love of God filled his heart, revealing an intelligent talented young man. His confused and sometimes naive state made for several rather amusing episodes.

Soon after arriving, Al was assigned to weed a recently planted section of Jerusalem artichokes. He was instructed as to which were weeds and which were not, and admonished to pull only weeds. When the foreman checked up on him the rows were straight. Every ragweed plant stood erect, and all the artichokes were gone! Some of the frustration and amusement was of Al's own doing, but others were setups fashioned by roommates and interns.

Back in the garden Al again toiled away--hopefully pulling out weeds this time. Gus, a young man assigned to oversee the work, spied a 4-inch PVC irrigation pipe that ran from near the building and ended not far from where Al was bent over in the garden. Not one to miss an opportunity for mischief, Gus lifted the pipe and in a deep sonorous voice spoke: "Al, this is God." Al looked up and initially attributed the phenomena to his fried brain. When the voice was heard plainly again, Al thought he was having his first religious experience! While this may sound like a cruel joke, Al knew how much Gus loved him and appreciated the prank as much as Gus did.

My son, Shawn, was also drawn to the lovable ex-con. They became friends despite the difference in age--and in experience. Shawn invited Al to go fishing with him, but Shawn needed to complete the job of resetting the nails that held down the corrugated roofing on the barn. Al volunteered to help. Between the two of them, they came up with the bright idea of strapping themselves together with thirty feet of rope. Al would work on one side of the peaked roof while Shawn worked on the other, thus eliminating the time-consuming effort of moving ladders. It was a disaster in the making. Shawn weighed 100 pounds and Al was now 250 pounds. You can guess the next scene in this Abbott and Costello routine! Al tripped and Shawn went flying up one side and down the other, bumping along over raised roofing nails. Scraped and embarrassed, the straightman and his fall-guy lay stacked in a heap of corn silage and fertilizer. A large one and a small one connected by the same line--I'd say there was already a pretty good string of mullets!

There comes a time in everyone's life when their faith is severely tested. It came early and painful for Al. He was still in the program when the call came for him from Lawrence and Memorial Hospital. I accompanied him to the morgue. Billy, Al's brother, had been shot while robbing a package store in Niantic. Al's mom was in no shape to handle it, so there was no one else to identify the body. Given Al's background, there were several ways he might be expected to react. He didn't respond to the challenges from old friends to get even and he didn't attempt to drown his grief in booze or drugs. He allowed God to be his Comforter. Al passed his first big test.

* * *

Warden Hill, a man with a reputation for being tough but honest, oversaw the prison where Al served his time. His policy was to never allow an ex-con back into the prison except to begin serving another term. But Al, a Class-B felon, was given permission to replace Michael as the Bible class leader in the Brooklyn Correctional Center. But allowing Al to reenter the prison was not the only first for Warden Hill. Acting as his "attorney," I represented Al before the Senior District Judge for the State of Connecticut. Al was requesting a complete pardon for his crimes. There were others there making the same plea, but everyone else applying for a pardon left with the same criminal record they came with. Court hours ground to a close and besides the judge and one clerk-of-the-court, only the two of us remained. "Will the petitioner approach the bench?" the clerk ordered.

On the judge's bench were two other recommendations for Al's pardon, besides Al's request and my recommendation. These had been submitted by the cop who had originally arrested Al, and from Warden Hill. This was the first and only time Warden Hill had spoken on behalf of an ex-con. The judge declared: "Pardon granted." Al could start his new life with a clean record--"Just as if he never..."

Twenty-five years after serving time in prison as a criminal, Al began serving time again--as a chaplain in New Hampshire State Prison. He continues to serve in that prison right up to this present time and is highly respected throughout New England. God uses the foolish things of this world to confound the wise.

*   *   *

Jackie carries on that same heritage. She had come to His Mansion steeped in drugs, alcohol, and prostitution--a life that could've landed her on the receiving end of the ladle she now extended to her friends. Like Al, life for Jackie has been a journey of picking her way through rough territory, but she's catching a great view today. The runaway retells the story from years earlier.

"Whoa...where ya goin'?" I grabbed her shirt so she couldn't keep running.

"Away from here...let go of me. Who do you think you are, you blankety-blank-blank-blank?"

"I'm Stan Farmer."

"So?" She retorted, annoyed that her intern was catching up to her.

"I'm the Executive Director of His Mansion."

"I don't care what you are. Let go of me!"

192

Jackie's first impression of me is vivid. I'm the blankety-blank that didn't let her run off the hill.

She wanted to do that a lot during her five years here and a couple times she did leave. The other times she got to struggle and argue about it with One whose title is senior to mine. Yet similarly, He won. "God told me I'd wasted enough of His time," Jackie explained. "He needed me to grow up fast because He had things He needed me to do." And He did.

The "Pit" is a stall beneath the barn where all the "you-know-what" is piled up. It's here that people in the program who have disregarded the rules find themselves doing "corrections." Free time is a highly valued commodity during ones stay in the community and losing any of it stings. "Creative circumstances" are arranged that involve the loss of free time while producing something of value, as consequences for unacceptable behavior. It is also here that Jackie picked up an important "degree" in her unique education! She was known for "speaking her mind" and smelling the results. Most residents as rowdy as Jackie would have been asked to leave. She did, in fact, bolt once, but God had other plans for her--things for her to do.

After leaving and returning, Jackie finally completed the program and went to serve as part of the team that tried to establish a program on Rum Cay in the Bahamas. From there it was to the streets of Boston, only this time not as a drug-numbed beggar, but as an angel of hope. Jackie went on to serve as Food Service Supervisor at the Boston Rescue Mission. It wasn't long before the "regulars" knew her by name. Running a food kitchen was not her first choice, but it got her where she could develop relationships with the lonely and the lost.

Jackie is still on the streets hanging out with derelicts, bums, and the homeless. She's still there, doing what God has for her to do. Only now she on the giving side. From her perspective today, Jackie has the vantage point--a unique view that few others get to enjoy.

XII ENCOURAGEMENT FOR
THE FINAL ASCENT

At the season of our lives when age and the wear-and-tear of the journey are taking their toll, when our vitality begins to ebb, the steepest cliffs and inclines may still be before us. More than youth and physical stamina is required for the final challenge. Wisdom, tempered by the experience we've gained through the arduous miles behind us, provides the keen edge that can be honed no other way. Stop to review the landscape that others and we have traversed--the rivers, canyons, potholes, and dead ends. Reminisce over the relationships that have been nurtured, the humorous stories, and the struggles we've come through together. Like the Hebrew people of old, it's vital we review and retell the victories over yesterday's challenges. This is our heritage.

Michener's historical novel, *The Covenant,* was fresh in my mind. I had just finished reading the book on the 20-hour flight from Boston to Johannesburg. During the past year the story of how God had established a healing community on a hill in New Hampshire had made its way to South Africa. Clinton Lester, a native South African, made the initial contact. Clinton was a part-time printer and a man who loved the Zulu people full-time. Although a white South African, Clinton speaks the Zulu tongue well enough to fool the Zulu tribesmen who fail to look up first. Clinton's son, Wayne, had fallen victim to South Africa's greatest internal threat. Not racial strife, but drugs.

Wayne had made the journey to His Mansion in New Hampshire and returned to his homeland with a burden and hope to bring another type of freedom to his beloved land. I was there at the request of his parents and others to explore the prospects of establishing a community for South Africans. This challenge carried me to Transvaal, Durban, Pretoria, Port Shepstone, Jo-berg, and Capetown.

While in Capetown I made the obligatory pilgrimage up Table Top Mountain. From there I took in the stunning panorama of the coastline from the southern tip of South Africa to the vast luscious vineyards in the north. The scene was so breathtaking that all I could do for the moment was to capture a mental photograph. Hopefully, the heart stopping gondola-ride back would not destroy the imagery. Once again on terra-firma the wonder of the mountaintop experience could be digested in a more relaxed setting.

The following day, I discovered a small cafe nestled halfway up the mountainside in the Sir Cecil Rhodes National Park. On a ledge cut into the side of the mountain, a few tables and a small kiosk provided hot rolls, and a cup of coffee that would please any Dutchman's palate. It satisfied mine.

Replaying my memory-tape from previous days mountaintop vista, I unloosed the history of Africa as I remembered it from Michener's book about the discovery, settlement, and cultivation of South Africa by the Dutch Reformers. The arrival of the British and the demeaning treatment of a proud people, reminiscent of the occupation of Ireland, India, and the Caribbean. I was moved with renewed appreciation for the brave American Patriots who stood against those same British armies in order to purchase America's freedom in 1776.

God brought together the most unlikely volunteers to walk together while I traveled throughout South Africa. The retired Chief Assayer of Africa's gold mines, an airline pilot, a printer, a recovering addict, and a formerly classified "colored" Indian from Capetown. Together, they believed God would provide a farm where down-and-outers, addicts, and lost men and women might find refuge. Wayne and his wife Tanya--a Bahamian girl who also served at His Mansion in New Hampshire--are the founding directors of a South African community located a hundred kilometers north of Johannisberg, which is modeled after His Mansion.

It is from these vantage points and reservoirs of history that one can gain the courage to turn again to the task before us and resume the final ascent. My memory volunteered several situations that in some respects made the "Dark Continent," seem very much like home. The bitterness lay just beneath the surface of my newfound Indian friend in Capetown--scars left by apartheid. Grand mansions adorn the hillsides overlooking abject poverty. And scrawny vagabonds, whose parents have been killed in tribal hatred, move about in the dark shadows of Johannisberg.

*   *   *

Before I met Steve I embraced the stereotypical perception that orphanages were located in Third World countries, like the African Continent--you know, places with severe overpopulation, poverty, and feudal struggles. It came as a shock to me to learn that such places existed in America. After all, every kid born in the U. S. has a home--don't they?

Steve was raised in the Cromwell's Children's Home in Connecticut, one of the most affluent states in the country. When he was brought to His Mansion, I jumped to the conclusion that his parents must have been killed in an accident or that he'd been discovered as an infant in the lady's room of the Hartford Civic Center during a senior prom, and then placed in an orphanage.

But Steve knew both of his parents. Neither of them was a criminal nor mentally or physically handicapped. He was placed in the home and had to process the reasons that he was there. The story turned out to be quite common--up to a point. Steve's parents were separated and Steve became unmanageable and was constantly in some sort of trouble in the community. Finally, the State had intervened and placed Steve in the "home."

Even being cared for by a loving staff couldn't keep the anger and rebellion in check. By age twelve, drugs and alcohol had become a part of Steve's life. At seventeen, he was forced onto the street from the only place that was ever home--a sad, and lonely day. There hadn't been many natural highs in his young life, so any direction he headed would be up.

God reveals Himself in many forms. It's not uncommon to see God in the eyes of a mother or godly pastor, but as Steve looks back he sees Him as a portly lady in a blue dress. Her name was Mae Simonsen and she was there for Steve's rescue.

Mae directed Cromwell's Children's Home and is one of God's faithful. Having no husband or family of her own, she transferred her considerable love onto youngsters like Steve. Mae Simonsen had heard about a place on a hill in New Hampshire and personally took Steve there.

The healing community in the mountains welcomed Steve. The ex-orphan took to the structured nature of his new environment like a duck to water. He had been raised on tight schedules and strict regimens and because of his diligence to routine, Steve was assigned the responsibility of stoking the furnaces during the nighttime hours. This meant that when everyone else was splitting and stacking wood, he slept!

This guy loved work and he loved to eat. At His Mansion, one is a prerequisite for the other. But when harvest season arrived, Steve wished he could accurately schedule his slothfulness. Zucchini seemed to make it to the menu far too often for his taste. He'd rather fake being sick than eat zucchini. Steve told me recently, "Talk about a colon cleanser! Zucchini in the morning, zucchini in the afternoon. To this day, I don't want my wife cooking zucchini...and it's been fifteen years!"

But His Mansion had more welcome effects on Steve. "All of my life my clothes had numbers on them...but there were no numbers here," he recalled. "The love that the interns gave at any given time--they were always there for me. Where else can you go where people work for love--for the Lord?"

Steve was not only loved and appreciated, but he was important to us. He made a contribution. While at His Mansion, Steve not only found a place and a family he discovered *his* place within a larger, eternal community. Today Steve is married and the father of two. He's teaching his wife and children how to be a family the way we taught him: love, and make sure everyone has meaningful responsibilities.

* * *

As you take a break in our journey and prepare for the final climb, enjoy the camaraderie that has developed. Consider those who have already overcome adversity and the heroes who have made it this far with you. Learn from those who've gone before. Offer encouragement to those left behind you.

From the steepest places there is nowhere to fall but down and should one stumble, it can be a long, deadly fall.

We tend to create heroes out of those who struggle from the very beginning in order to get to the top because most of us identify with them. Ironically, there's not nearly as much appreciation, or sympathy, for the privileged individual who, we perceive, enjoyed a privileged start and then subsequently falls. In reality, it may take more courage for the person who has made it to this point without pain or difficulty who suffers a catastrophic reversal, to acknowledge the failure and begin again. Shelley knows what this is all about.

"Oh, my gosh, I think I'm going to die!" Shelley was sure she had been condemned to Stalag 13. Nearly every aspect of life in this community was foreign to her. There were no sidewalks, no maid and no mom to meet her every need. It was so different from her past. It's a wonder she ever learned to talk around the silver spoon that was stuck in her mouth. Olympic swimming pools, plush gardens, doting parents, summer schools, music lessons, private schools, special tutors, and orthodontists were inherent in her social setting.

Shelley and her sisters had lived in London and in elite New York City suburbs. They summered at their parents' estate in the Green Mountains, when they weren't traveling abroad. Life for Shelley began upon the hill of wealth and privilege.

In the middle of what should have been the most joyous, fun-filled years of her youth--the very time when all the privilege and wealth could be taken full advantage of--Shelley came under the spell of a terrible demon named Anorexia Nervosa.

Seeking a cure for this life-threatening condition, her parents engaged the best medical and psychological help available in Europe and in the United States, to no avail. Shelley would be led out of the valley of the shadow of death to another hill where the radiance of hope would drive the shadows away.

200

Shelley, like Orphan Steve, turned the corner into the tree-lined dirt road and discovered herself in this "enchanted community." It is true, as they say, that "beauty is in the eye of the beholder," because the picture appeared quite different to Shelley than it did to Steve!

Within days of Shelley's arrival, she was cleaning toilets, dusting bookshelves, and feeling thoroughly overwhelmed. She never envisioned herself picking potato bugs off leaves and depositing them in cans of kerosene only to watch them writhe in the pangs of death. It was refreshing to learn that her father was amused to envision his debutante daughter getting grubby and dirty while completing chores her sisters were never required to perform. Within months, the monster that had been stealing her life was being driven away.

This seventeen-year-old frightened girl with the nervous giggle was shocked to find herself with little power to influence others. She had no staff to perform life's unpleasant tasks and was at the mercy of a company of practitioners who had very little professional qualifications--at least that she could detect. This unpredictable and uncontrollable situation opened the door for transformation.

Lifesaving change could be purchased only in a currency foreign to her. She had no purchasing power until she exchanged her goals for someone else's. Having purchased a new agenda she could afford to say "no" to the old voices urging her to serve an unseen evil master, or to perform in order to meet others' expectations.

Twelve months after her arrival on the hill, a new person--a transformed woman--left the hill to reenter her family's world. During her stay at His Mansion, Shelley completed her high school education in time to formally graduate from the private preparatory high school that she had dropped out of a year earlier. She was also accepted into the university of her choice.

Shelley now enjoys working in different kinds of gardens. The potentially beautiful creations she finds there, are also being attacked by another form of disease and infestation. Her work in this new environment is not unlike the work that was so repulsive to her on the hill. She has a passion for working with the hurting and disenfranchised youngsters who are growing up in the ghettos of our big cities. Her university studies will help equip Shelley to make a difference.

*   *   *

A woman in an army officer's uniform zooming past my office window on a motorcycle distracted my thoughts. Curious, I rushed outside and waved the Kawasaki to a halt on its return trip down the hill. No, I hadn't been dreaming; it was a U. S. Army officer on a motorcycle. This was to be more than a passing visit. It was what I've come to describe as a "Divine encounter."

Lt. Susan Bertram had arranged a transfer to the nearby National Guard unit so she could be close to her mom. Her dad had recently passed away and Sue was on her way to visit her at her lakeside cabin. The sign, at the entrance of His Mansion's driveway, had caught her attention.

The impetus for noticing the sign was a recent dream. She'd been counseled at a dream seminar that she attended: "Pockets of people will survive and your out-in-space friends will help you communicate. You'll be led to a hidden valley in Vermont."

We were, indeed, a "pocket of people" and some of us were pretty "spacey," but this was not Vermont. It was New Hampshire. Oh well, it was close enough for government work, I guess! She drove in, not intending to talk with anyone. But she did, and she was back a week later for a second look.

After her tour, Sue visited with me in my office and was surprisingly open about her past. I explained how my life was changed as the result of an experience I'd had while I was in the Submarine Service. Socially and economically our backgrounds were much the same. We'd both been brought up as Catholics and alcoholism had played a major role in our families.

Sue's grief over the loss of her dad was obvious, as was the concern for her mother's welfare. Her siblings were also going through difficulties. But there was more, Sue was depressed, directionless, and short on hope to carry her through this rough period.

I didn't know enough about her or her circumstances to have confidence in any advice I might offer and I was also well aware of my limitations as a counselor. I suggested we pray. To my surprise she agreed, but I could tell she didn't have a clue what was going on. I prayed for her and asked if she'd like to pray. When she opened her mouth to pray her voice faltered, but her heart took over. She wept. When she did speak, it was to acknowledge her need for God.

Sue recognized the spiritual maturity possessed by Vivian, my assistant, and sought her out as a mentor. She attended a Bible study taught by Viv, and the two became lifelong friends. As Sue puts it, "She raised me."

A year passed as Sue worked to pay off her debts and completed her monthly National Guard obligation. Under Viv's tutelage, Sue grew emotionally and spiritually. Six months later she was asked to serve in the His Mansion community as an intern. She remembers her early days in housekeeping vividly: "I was in the military and had 40 men working for me and then all of a sudden, I'm kneeling here scrubbing toilet bowls." On her knees at one toilet she told God, "This is so humiliating. This is so humbling." She wondered what kind of hope could emerge from a toilet.

It was humbling for Sue, but after ten months of menial tasks, including training at "the bowl," she was asked to take responsibility for several young ladies who had come to the community with serious emotional problems. From there, Sue rose to Senior Mentor. She enjoyed her new role and was great at meeting parents, talking to pastors, and helping new staff women get through those tough moments that were all too familiar to her.

We usually think of stuff going *down* the toilet, but for Sue, the porcelain bowl was a fountain of blessing and surprise. One evening, "Follow the Clues," a popular evening recreation game was in progress. Sue's clues led her to the spot in the bathroom where she'd once argued with God. When she looked into the bowl, she discovered a live frog with an engagement ring tied around its nearly nonexistent neck. She'd soon be kneeling at an altar instead.

Roy McCandless, a third-year law student at Harvard, had taken a one-year break to serve at His Mansion. At the end of his commitment, Roy returned to Harvard in body and mind; his heart remained at His Mansion with Sue!

A year later, Roy reflected on his time at His Mansion, in an article that appeared in *Christian Legal Society.* "My painless decision [to serve at His Mansion] became a painful reality. There I sat in a room full of suffering men. I was the scalpel, their hearts were the patients, and God was the surgeon. There was only one problem: no anesthesia."

But the Surgeon was operating on Roy as well. He soon realized how much he mirrored these men. "Each of them in some way was dealing with the same issues I was," Roy explained as he remembered the clown and the one with the low self-esteem. The difference? He had chosen socially acceptable addictions.

As he wrote in an article in <u>Christian Legal Society</u> : "Drugs and alcohol have never attracted me, but I was an addict to the lure of success and human achievement. Having served at His Mansion for 11 months, I can now say that I am not becoming a lawyer because I must somehow make my mark on the world or store up treasures in the bank. I'm becoming a lawyer because Jesus has freed me to serve others and to help meet their legal needs."

*   *   *

Another top-notch student who became a valuable guide to others was Dave, who grew up an English-speaking Quebecois. "You're white, male, and a Christian. You're gonna have to be twice as good as anybody else." Dave knew his professor was correct. Even though he was in the top social work Ph.D. program in the United States, he had three strikes against him. Not all of Dave's hardships were issued at birth, however. Failing grades and antics such as throwing an apple at the board in the middle of class got him kicked out of his community college.

Three years after his expulsion, Dave headed south to New Hampshire to a community he'd heard about, called His Mansion. He wanted to have a "hands on" experience with God, rather than a vicarious one experienced as a financial donor. Within weeks of his arrival, the word among the students was, "The only reason Dave is on staff is that he was too rebellious to be student!" Maybe it's my time in the military that makes me respect the observations of the "enlisted" folks. In many aspects they were correct!

Due to Dave's trade skills, he worked alone, personally determining the order of his tasks. Having hauled his tools to a staff person's residence to do some brief repairs on their heater, he notified the lady of the house of his intent, "I'd like to come down and do this job on the furnace. I'm gonna shut the power off for a couple of hours. It's kind of a cold, windy day and the temperature might drop a few degrees in the building. Just so you're aware that it's gonna happen." Helen deferred to her husband, instructing the maintenance man to clear it with him. Her husband also happened to be Dave's boss.

Dave called. But his boss replied, "Well, its pretty cold out there today. Why don't you wait?"

205

"I was ripped," Dave admitted. As he went to retrieve his tools, he thought, "See when I get back to *this* job! Who is this character to tell me what to do?"

For three days, Dave nursed his grudge. Talking over the situation with his mentor, Dave was asked to consider the issue of obedience. Dave tried to explain, "But I am obedient. I did exactly what he asked me to do. I walked away from that job."

Over a decade later, the once defensive learner remembers his mentor's response, "What is God more concerned with, outward actions or the attitude of the heart?" As he considered that question, he also answered another. Who was this guy to tell him what to do? "He was my boss, a director, and it was his house." Of all the folks, he was the very person who did have the right to tell him what to do!

Over the next two years, as Dave learned to live this lesson, he was gradually entrusted with the mentoring of residents and the supervision of other interns. Something had happened somewhere!

During that time, Dave was asked to switch mentors. Unhappy with the proposal, Dave was reticent to open up to Mike. But the Dartmouth grad became his supervisor and mentor nonetheless. To the first direct question Mike asked, Dave answered, "I don't really feel I can answer this question because I'm just not sure I trust and respect you as an individual."

"Well, tell me about it."

Dave replied, "You're filled with pride. And when you're playing sports and losing, you blow up. It's like you're a little kid."

"Yeah. Yeah. I can see that."

Michael heard him out and admitted that Dave was right. No argument, just acceptance. Never before had Dave confronted anyone about anything serious and gotten such a response! Contrary to their cultural bias, Dave and Mike became good friends.

Dave had become a strong advocate of community, but one of his charges was not so keen. Derik's parents were hippies, and they'd fed him drugs as a child. He'd had a rough go of it at the Mansion, but he was making it. A six-month stay is no small accomplishment. But when Derik announced that he wanted to leave, no amount of coaxing or reasoning could make him change his mind.

On the inevitable trip to the bus station, Dave asked his student, "Derik, tell me truthfully... why do you feel it's best to leave?" Knowing he'd soon be on a bus, he admitted,

All my life I've known nothing but hurt, pain, and ridicule. I've been made fun of and put down. That's what I know. That's what I feel comfortable with. I'm here and for the first time in my life, I'm feeling happiness, I'm feeling joy. I don't know how to handle it. Those things really scare me...They scare me so much that I'd rather be in an environment that I know.

For some, the fact that they have progressed so far--farther than they ever thought they might--is frightening. To turn toward the final climb is to risk losing it all, at least from their perspective. My heart goes out to the Deriks of this world.

Every day after lunch, Phil turned his chair around and stared out the window for fifteen minutes. No movement. Just a stare. This is not an uncommon state for many residents as they enjoy a few idle moments, but his was disturbingly distant--and different. When the allotted break between the meal and workcrew had passed, Phil got up and reported for duty. Nothing seemed to pierce the depression that hovered over him--except for his prayers.

God, I realize that I'm in depression and I need to get out of it. I need to know that you really love me. I feel abandoned by you; that you don't love me. I've just *got* to know; *got* to know that You love me. At the same time I realize that because I'm enveloped in this shroud of depression there's no way that you can tell me that you love me--it would never get through.

There are two people that I trust and respect on the hill. Perhaps, if you would just please tell one of them to tell me that you've heard this prayer and that you love me...

A couple days passed as Phil waited.

Then one of those two people, now one of the mentoring supervisors, approached Dave; "This is really strange Dave, but I feel God's just told me I should tell Phil God loves him and that I love him too. Is it okay if I go up and tell him that?"

"Yeah, sure. Go ahead." Dave replied.

This specific answer to prayer brought Phil out of his depression. For Dave, it affirmed that community and the relationships it fosters are essential. It is those relationships that many Mansion alumni miss the most, and Dave is no exception. But rather than lamenting what he lacks, he's striving to recreate it by building relationships with each of his thirteen classmates at George Washington University.

Dave was encouraged by a professor's answer to a question he posed at the end of a term: "What's it been like getting to know an evangelical?"

"No offense, but getting to know you has been like getting to know a child molester and then learning that he's all right after all!" replied his professor.

The strikes are against him, but why such a terrible analogy? Dave is a straight, white, Christian male, boldly representing his Messiah at the doctoral level of thoroughly secular Washington University.

I failed to see the full potential in this cocky young man when he first arrived on staff at His Mansion. Charlie Delano, my high school principal with the size fourteen shoe, saw more "stuff" in me than I saw in Dave--but thankfully, God is never hindered by my lack of insight.

The brash individual who could hardly take "no" for an answer when fixing a furnace isn't with us as we face the final ascent. He underwent a metamorphosis a ways back and now he has an MCS, MSW, and finishing his Ph.D. so that he can credibly integrate faith in God with social work. By tackling such a tough course and succeeding, Dave has become an inspiration to the rest of us as we begin the final ascent.

The experience and lessons we learn, we get to keep. The friends and precious relationships we've built, we get to keep. The confidence in the truth that we shall overcome and reach the summit, we get to keep. These are the energy-boosters that help propel us upward. The mistakes, disappointments, disillusionments, dead ends, and misery, all these we can leave behind. To hold on to them will only slow us down and make the final ascent painful. The Apostle, St. Paul, says it well:

No, dear friends, I am still not all I should be, but I am focusing all my energies on this one thing: Forgetting the past and looking forward to what lies ahead, I strain to reach the end of the race and receive the prize for which God, through Jesus Christ, is calling us to heaven.

XIII. PRIZE AT THE TOP

Since the moment we set our eyes toward the summit, an invisible Guide has been beside us. The closer we get to the goal, the more profoundly we sense His presence. He was there when we stumbled and fell. He was there to witness our heroic sprints. He was there when those whom we thought were committed dropped out. The Observer was there not to criticize, judge, or condemn. Rather, He has been silently encouraging and cheering us on. When we finally cross the finish line, He'll be there to embrace us and to whisper in our ears, "Well done!"

One of my favorite professors in the school of life was a damsel named Susie, my son's 4-H project--a Jersey heifer. Soft brown features, doe-like eyes, and a personality that signaled the capacity for affection.

Susie was pregnant and her time was at hand. We prayed for another heifer that could one day provide additional milk for the community. On sunny days, Susie would lie against the outside wall of the shed, retreating inside at nightfall. I enjoyed greeting her each morning as I left for the Mansion and Susie appreciated the affection that a scratch afforded.

The sun had been up for only a few minutes, but Susie was already in her usual spot. I reached through the fence and touched her neck. Instantly I recognized that something was very wrong. Her body was deathly cold. I shouted for Shawn. I knew this would be a hard lesson, but it was all part of the 4-H experience.

Jerseys, like their sister breed, Guernseys, are susceptible to a condition known as milk fever. The expectant mother diverts so much nutrition into her milk in anticipation of feeding her newborn that she deprives herself and goes into shock. If the condition is not immediately treated she will die, but if sucrose is injected directly into the jugular vein then the mother can often be revived.

We had the supplies, and Shawn knew the routine. He had learned his 4-H lessons well and took over like a seasoned veterinarian. Several minutes after the fluid had been injected, Susie's skin began to warm and little involuntary shivers rippled across her hide. Signs of life!

No sooner had she shown signs of life, than she began to give birth. Shawn and I, acting as midwives, helped her give birth to a delicate lovely heifer. The mother, however, had given her all. The effort was too great for her weakened condition. With her head bent tightly back across her side, she died.

The colostrum in a mother's milk, soon after birth, contains high concentrations of minerals and natural antibiotics to keep the newborn healthy until it can make it on its own. So with a heavy heart, Shawn milked the precious fluid from the now deceased mother. Using a baby's bottle, he fed the new arrival.

The calf survived and eventually won the First Prize blue ribbon at the Woodstock Fair. Eventually, the family at His Mansion would share her prize when refreshed with her rich milk.

*   *   *

In the course of my journey, I've had the honor of interacting with fellow travelers that have been crushed by folks whom they loved and trusted--people who had head-on collisions with their own lousy choices. For some, chance and circumstance took its toll. It is not uncommon for souls under extreme duress to simply want to lie down and die.

You may one day find yourself in such a spot--take heart. There is often a point as you're nearing the top when you become so exhausted that you don't think you can go another step. Stop! This is the time to take an assessment of your own journey, see how far you've come, and listen for the voice of encouragement. There is a Physician handy who will administer the sucrose necessary to revive you. He will not leave you. He will not abandon you. Your victory is assured. The prize is within reach.

*   *   *

Elmien is one of the travelers I've met along the way who can attest to the Great Physician's loving care and healing power. He brought her back from the brink of death and gave her a vision of the prize.

"According to the doctors, Elmien's only got six months to live." News that the distraught mother had not voiced at

213

home was being unburdened with a friend. Unbeknownst to mom, her nine-year-old daughter overheard that conversation. Mom, Elmien's resident expert, was saying that she would die--that her life would probably end before she reached ten.

Elmien's family had recently moved from Zululand to dad's new post in a National Reserve in South Africa. Life and death was as close as her backyard. For hours, predator and prey in perfect play, she would watch even while one ate another to survive. Now she understood that she was the one who would be consumed. Her predator, *aplastic anemia fanconi*, was subtle in sabotage. It kept her body from healing itself. Bruises from insignificant bumps festered for months. She could hardly conquer her enemy's name, let alone its attack.

Two months after Elmien overheard the secret, a pastor visited her home. He came because Elmien and her siblings had been coming to church. She found the Sunday morning ritual to be confusing and was annoyed that those who mandated that she go, insisted on staying home. They least understand the Elizabethan prose, but it was gibberish to her.

The day the pastor came to her house his question was simple: "If you die today, where are you going?" He had knowledge of her disease-induced life sentence, so he felt comfortable talking with her about eternity. At the end of three hours of dialogue, Elmien gave control of her life to God.

Elmien had been prey long before the genetic timebomb exploded. Some time prior to her conversion, Elmien met with her best friend who sensed the enemy's presence and expressed her observation to Elmien saying, "You've been abused, tell me about it." Elmien poured out her account of the physical, emotional, and sexual abuse that plagued her past. Alcohol was her father's god and while serving it, he had sacrificed an appropriate relationship with his daughter.

The disease had not progressed as quickly as predicted and Elmien entered her teen years. As is true for some mothers of adolescents, Elmien's mother occasionally read her youngest child's mail. The words of one particular letter written to a friend told her what her fourteen-year-old could not. Her husband, Mr. de Jager, had hurt their "baby." How aptly the family surname depicted her husband: de Jager is Dutch for "the chaser!"

Immediately after his wife confronted Mr. de Jager, informing him that she was aware of the inappropriate treatment of their daughter, he was compelled by duty to head off on another wilderness trip in the vast game reserve. When he returned after a couple of days, Elmien feared for her life. The abuse had been difficult. Childhood, purity, and wholeness had all been irrevocably defiled, but now maiming was no longer the goal. This diagnosed psychopath evoked new levels of fear in his daughter. She'd known the fear before as she struggled in the talons of disease, but now the predator was personified. To her horror, it bore the face of her father. She lived without hope that the situation might end.

Eighteen months later, Mr. and Mrs. de Jager went to church with their children for the first time. That day they both surrendered to Christ. The Holy Spirit had become "the chaser," and they had been caught. The physical harm to their children stopped abruptly. God had taken up residence in the heart of the predator.

One evening, four months later, Elmien attended a concert at her church. As she sat in the bubble of her friends, she realized that God was speaking to her. The control she had relinquished to God six years earlier was tentative, leaving friends as her main support. As she sat with her friends in the balcony, she sensed God was asking her to follow Him "no matter what." Still seeking control over her life, she argued, "What would my friends think?"

Moments later, the speaker looked straight into the gallery where she was sitting and said, "You know you need to come down...forget about your friends and family. You know that your life isn't right with God." Jolted out of her internal banter by the outside voice that seemed to have joined it, she got up out of her seat and walked to the front of the church to do business with the Lord.

During an eight-hour drive with her parents to a conference advertised as "Love Southern Africa," Elmien mused about the future. She asked God, "If I get nothing else out of this missions conference, God, would you show me where to go and when?" Two hours later, as they stood in a crowd, a stranger turned around and said, "OM, next year." Operation Mobilization is a missions organization specializing in short-term experiences for young adults. The idea excited Elmien and she chose to commit. During her orientation with OM, a speaker challenged, "How do you see God?" Although she was unable to complete the exercise of imagining herself in God's lap, she did have a vision:

A three- or four-year-old girl was in an orchard, curiously following a man down one of the rows. When the man realized he had a little shadow, he turned around. Seeing him turn, the toddler darted behind one of the trees. Peeking out from her hideaway, she could see him squatting on his haunches with his arms outstretched. At eye level with his new friend, his gesture was inviting. His smile was welcoming. But after a time of looking at the tuft of hair sticking out from behind the fruit tree, his expression changed. Tears came. Still the little one refused to move from her refuge. Elmien believed she was that child and Jesus was that man.

A friend of a friend worked in a healing community for those who struggled with issues like Elmien's. Would she be interested? Due to a growing awareness that she knew God as her Friend, Savior, and Lord, but not as her Father, Elmien agreed to check it out. Receiving literature, she was surprised to learn that His Mansion was not even in the Republic of South Africa!

There was a flurry of applications, e-mails, faxes, and phone calls. She had a heart for the nations of the world, but not America! Money was an honest argument since she didn't have 5500 Rand to purchase a transatlantic ticket. But when her account balance read R5700, an anonymous and unexpected deposit, that excuse was no longer an option.

The contradictory declarations coming from the American consulate created another hitch. The Monday before her scheduled Friday flight, Elmien called again. Was it worth the five-hour drive to Johannesburg? Could she board the plane with any confidence that she'd be allowed to stay at its final destination? The answer was yes! So after eleven months of correspondence, complications, and arguments with God, Elmien left the RSA for the USA.

It was on her twenty-first birthday and during a nine-hour wait for a postponed flight, she made an entry in her journal that began:

Yesterday I left my beloved country. My parents, brother, sister, and friends were at the airport to see me off. It was a sad affair for a birthday--a 21st birthday at that. It was a day like any other in most ways, yet a day so different to any other I'd ever known.

And ended:

I wonder how many others have stood at this point, maybe sat on this very bench, realizing that the life of a child is gone forever, knowing that there's no turning back. Knowing that the only road leads forward over rocky, mountainous terrain. Knowing God is still sovereign and he holds me in the palm of his mighty hand.

Father God, once again I realize my weakness, my dependence on you. And again I pray: "Lord, I believe, help my unbelief..."

Belief. Elmien had seen God provide. It was no minor miracle that she was alive. He provided even when she didn't ask and in ways that seemed unbelievable: a stranger offering a direct answer to prayer, mysterious bank deposits, and visa headaches cleared. So why did she doubt?

Elmien's fragile faith is understandable when I recall the Biblical record. The same folk who walked safely across the dry riverbed of the Red Sea, whined about not having drinking water three days later. Or more recently, one who witnessed God answer prayer and supplied funds for a move to New Hampshire, made a phone call to ensure that finances would be there to pay for a house being delivered by truck! God is patient with His people. Elmien became a vital member of the healing community and once the fact of God's faithfulness sank in, a gifted young pilgrim emerged. Elmien had what it took to rise out of the ashes, and live again. She is living proof that this same hope is available for all of us.

* * *

Praising God for answered prayer, inspiring other's faith, and encouraging the frustrated seems easier to do for the strangers I interact with along the way than for those who are near and dear. The ultimate test comes, it seems, when the person in need is our spouse, parent, or children.

There was a time when I feared the uphill grade was too much for me. I had no pat answers. It was a trail I'd never blazed before. I felt so helpless, and rightly so, because it was our son's journey, not mine, yet, Joan and I had to walk it with him--and trust. God was faithful when I had all but given up, but the Guide was there; I sensed His presence.

Shawn had a paper route when he was twelve and had tripped while crossing a field to the next customer, a small motel. He had fallen on a broken bottle and his eye was bleeding as he entered the motel.

An ambulance rushed him to Lawrence and Memorial Hospital where an eye specialist gave us the shocking prognosis: "Your son is going to lose his left eye." The fluid had ebbed from his eye sack and was not regenerative. The call went out for prayer. Friends and strangers prayed and prayed. As "chance" would have it, New England's premier eye surgeon was lecturing at the hospital. He was demonstrating a then new technology called laser surgery. He took on Shawn's case. Three days later the bandages were removed. The sack was refilling by itself, which the doctors labeled as "quite remarkable."

The most optimistic predictions that experts could offer was that Shawn would not be able to see out of the damaged eye, but that the blind eye would have definition and therefore, would not subject him to the pain and stigma of an empty socket. A year later Shawn tested 20/20 vision in both eyes! Six years later, he would pass a physical to enter the U. S. Navy. This crisis, and God's intervention, laid the foundation for enduring even greater tragedies.

Shawn returned home two years after enlisting. His hopes of serving aboard nuclear submarines, as I had, were dashed by the discovery of the laser scar on his eye which had not been spotted during prior physical examinations.

Joan and I had grown spiritually by witnessing the miraculous healing of Shawn's eye. The accident that had nearly cost the use of an eye was one that came in a moment and was not caused by careless actions on his part. It is easier to endure this kind of innocent, inadvertent catastrophe, than the damage and pain resulting from irresponsible life-style choices. Joan and I were to learn that life in a small town could be as detrimental to some as life in big cities is for others. It was for Shawn.

Shawn acquired a student loan and attended a state technical institute. Partying, drinking, and smoking dope--mostly driven by restlessness--became his method of dealing with the boredom. Parents must stand by and watch the painful process, often having little power to change things.

His life-style never affected his ability or ambition for physical labor. He worked hard all the time. He married a local girl that he had gone to high school with, and the following year our grandson, Seth, was born. But married life for the young couple was tumultuous during those first years. From where I stood, it looked like a prolonged plane wreck! Loud outbursts, airborne appliances, and slammed doors was evidence of the young couple's frustration with the responsibilities of married life. Excessive drinking and smoking pot were a part of Shawn's daily routine. His mother and I were frantic most of the time, which drove us to pray, pray, pray.

I'd never felt so helpless, even though I'd watched other parents deal with similar situations. My only son's life was going down the toilet and I feared for my new grandson. I was actually reluctant to get to know this little guy, because I didn't think I could handle the pain of the inevitable loss.

With little planning or forethought, Shawn took his family to Maine and moved his wife and child into a 16-foot dilapidated camp trailer on a lot deep in the Maine woods, that I deeded to him. The heartache for Joan and me was palpable.

We visited them periodically and grieved each time. They had no running water, electricity, or proper sewerage. Candles provided their only light. Seth slept in a cradle in a dark corner. Shawn was gone much of the day. Joan and I imagined far worse than was reality. It was awful!

The cracker box trailer was set up next to the foundation of a 200-year-old farmhouse that had long since been carted away or buried. Tons of fieldstone, mostly covered with trees and underbrush, littered the ground. Each day Shawn would emerge from his "Appalachian condo" and work to uncover all that was left of the old homestead. Soon he had pile upon pile of fieldstone of every size and shape surrounding the camper. He claimed to be studying how the original builders had built with stone and informed us he was planning for his future, which would be building with stone. I told him I thought *he was* stoned!

The coming of winter drove the threesome out of the woods and into an apartment on Monjoy Hill in Portland, Maine. He found work with a contractor building a bridge over the saltwater channel connecting Portland to Falmouth. High-walking steel and volunteering to ride the cable hanging from a crane, Shawn challenged death. It seemed as if he either didn't care to live or didn't believe he could die. To make matters worse, he drank heavily during the workday and performed those risky tasks under the influence of alcohol.

Growing responsibilities paralleled his increased addiction. His helplessness was manifesting itself in depression and he had problems making healthy decisions. Joan and I feared it was only a matter of time or circumstance before Shawn would take his life, or lose it, leaving behind a young wife and a beautiful son. Joan and I prayed--by faith placing them in God's hands--and waited.

There are times in life when no more warnings can be issued, no more advice is welcomed, and parents are completely helpless to make a son or daughter believe differently. Nothing in my experience with emotionally tormented parents had adequately prepared me for this heart-wrenching drama. Joan and I prepared to lose our son, our daughter-in-law, and our grandson. Separation and divorce were inevitable and imminent. With it would go any confidence that we would be a part of our new grandson's life.

At times like these, even those indifferent toward religion might resort to prayer. Being people who had years ago cast our hopes upon the God of Hope, we continued to bathe that hope in prayer. Meanwhile, Shawn worked and drank, drank and worked, smoked and drank! Our children were adults. We had seen them successfully out of the nest. This was the time when parents look forward to breathing easier and enjoying grandchildren. We had come so far and now it looked as if all might be lost. Where was the hope? There was no sign of the prize but it was there in the fog and rain, just out of sight.

It was a bitter night--windy, rainy, miserable, and just short of ice. The phone rang as we were preparing to go to bed--it was Shawn! Every call was filled with frightening possibilities. What would it be this time?

"I need help. I've got to do something, I'm losing my family, my life...."

"I'll be there," I interrupted. "Where are you? I'm coming for you!"

Shawn said, "No," with a voice that signaled certainty. He would be at our house when he got there--somehow. They had no car and it sounded as if he was coming alone.

In the cold, early morning hours Shawn arrived at our door. The prodigal son had returned. Oh, what joy filled our hearts! There were many unanswered questions, but not tonight. This was a time to love.

Soon thereafter, Shawn, Sharon, and wonderful Seth moved into a single room in the rear of the community's chapel and became resident church mice. Shawn became the sawyer, running our Woodmizer saw mill, producing lumber for His Mansion's expansion. The Great Physician was working on the young contractor as he sharpened blades, did maintenance, and worked with fellow strugglers. This became a time of healing and reconciliation for Shawn.

When Shawn finished his stint in His Mansion's program, he went to work at a nearby paper mill. This was a time of healing and recovery for the couple. Life was taking on a healthier routine. There were signs of healing in his marriage, too. Shawn and his growing family, now with two sons, moved out of the His Mansion campus and into an apartment near the mill in Antrim. We held our breath.

Shawn and a friend were riding his 350 Honda to his apartment where dinner awaited them when a 100-pound black Labrador shot out of the brush and into the roadway in front of them. Shawn was not wearing a helmet, a sign of lingering poor judgment. His face was buried in the instrument panel and then he surfed 60 feet of blacktop on his face and chest! His nose was flattened badly, his teeth demolished, and the skin of his chest and belly ground off. The ambulance carried him to the hospital in a coma.

Joan and I received the news upon our arrival in Michigan, where I had a speaking engagement. We immediately flew back to New Hampshire, but we were warned not to hold out hope for our son's survival. Here we were again!

There is no point in pretending one can describe the devastation we felt, Yet we were not alone. We called everyone we knew who might uphold us in prayer. People all over the world once again checked in on our behalf.

Shawn woke up and began the healing process. He had suffered skull damage, and there was severe hemorrhaging on the brain. Holes were tapped and clots of blood vacuumed out. The aftereffects of severe head trauma are well recognized, one of which is a sense of immortality. Careless and reckless behavior was a problem before the accident. We had no idea what would happen now. The real test of Shawn's recovery from his previous life-style had begun.

The weeks passed by slowly. One of the most personally painful and humbling experiences for Shawn was allowing me to lather his face and shave him so his neck brace didn't chafe. He loved me, but the helplessness attacked his manhood. Tears would form and anger would radiate from his eyes.

Finally, he was able to return to work at the mill. His restlessness soon returned and Shawn announced that he was quitting the mill and going into business for himself. His business would be working with stone!

Oh, no! I thought. *Here we go again!* But my judgment was way off. "Stone Wall Landscaping" was a success from day one. Today Shawn is a Master Mason specializing in free-standing, mortarless stone construction--walls, fireplaces, chimneys, and houses! Some of the grandest manses outlying New York City display his handiwork. As improbable as his success appeared to be at that time, Joan and I now shout praises from the mountaintop!

*   *   *

When a loved one is transported out of a seemingly fatal situation, we eagerly lift our hearts in praise. But it is when one goes beyond the miracle of healing to become an agent of healing, that our praises soar. These experiences are wonderful foreshadows of the greater prize.

Though often painful to relatives and friends--certainly disconcerting to those who have not found hope and purpose for living--when a loved one leaves this temporary journey to begin the eternal. In ways that we cannot fully grasp, they have claimed The Prize.

*   *   *

Dotty Christensen sensed the presence of the Guide earlier than the rest of us. When God was about to begin the adventure we know as the Church, a group of 120 gathered on a rooftop. There was a smaller, closer group of 72 within the larger one. Among the 72 there were three--Peter, James, and John--who were the "inner circle." But there was one whose relationship to the Guide was unique. John snuggled up to Jesus. Dotty reminds me of John. She loved Jesus and couldn't wait to embrace Him.

Some of the encouragement we receive along the way comes from the troupe we've traveled with the longest. We grow close with some of our companions. They become like family and we expect to be arriving at the summit about the same time. But occasionally a preview of the prize ahead seems

224

to energize certain individuals and they kick it up to a sprint, reaching their eternal goal earlier than we expected. When this happens, we're hurt--sometimes even a little angry--but we'll see 'em soon! Miss Dot is one of those companions who claimed a piece of everyone's heart.

Dotty became a close friend and central figure in our community. "Miss Dot," as she was often called, was an un-married, career schoolteacher that taught in Northeastern Connecticut for many years. Through a lifelong friend, she was introduced to her ultimate best friend and it changed her life. Not long after her new birth, Dotty began attending a course on biblical counseling that I taught on the porch of His Mansion in Connecticut. She was more excited than the other students and had an insatiable appetite for all things spiritual.

The day after the Connecticut fire, Dotty made her log cabin home available to several displaced staffers, and her love for His Mansion was cemented. Over lunch at Zip's Diner, in Dayville, Connecticut, I proposed to Dotty--well, sort of. I asked her if she would be willing to leave her teaching career, log cabin, and friends to come with us to New Hampshire and teach the young women. There was no hesitation. "Yes!" she said.

While Dotty cut no slack when it came to what God had to say about life, she could keep a roomful laughing with her witty puns and humorous twists of phrases. The evidence of her quick sense of humor and upbeat attitude was every-where she worked: Personal tutoring for GEDs (General Equivalency Diplomas), Bible classes, and any kind of sports. Dot was in the middle of everything.

Dotty could be confrontational (her many years as a physical education teacher prepared her for that), but she had a soft heart for hurting women. On family fun nights another side of her was enjoyed by all. "Allemande left. Ladies to the right, men to the left." Dotty would bring out her collection of vintage 78rpm square-dance records and call the dance. Square dances were a lively addition to the His Mansion family life, thanks to Dotty.

Everyone was shocked and saddened when we learned that Dotty had breast cancer because Dotty was the most loved woman on the hill. Mastectomy was the first punch and had set her up for a right cross. Cancer was soon found in her lymph nodes. Chemotherapy, radiation, sickness, and hair loss all followed. The results were not encouraging and Dotty announced that she'd not continue treatment. She loved her Lord and would wait for Him to call her.

Penny, His Mansion's office manager, was Dotty's "best bud." She would bring her meals, laugh, sit, and talk with her. During a surprise birthday party that her roommates had planned for Penny; Penny stole away to Dotty's little apartment. When she walked into the living room, Penny discovered Dotty lying down with her wig propped on the back of the couch. Dotty was always careful to look her best, so this was a rare moment. For a few seconds, an awkward tension hung in the air, but Dotty broke out in laughter. The wig remained on the couch.

Mary Moore, another special friend of Dot's, sat with Dotty on another night and as they read and sang together, it became obvious Dotty was failing. Mary called me and together we sang and prayed as Dotty quietly left our company to join a much livelier party in heaven.

There are still times, especially during the late fall and early winter, when I look out of my office window and imagine seeing a white-haired lady dressed in dark blue slacks and a powder blue sweater trudging up the road with a slight forward lean. Dotty was a source of unwavering faith and strength. When she was a part of an activity she brought with her a positive, upbeat dynamic, but also a standard that would not be compromised. When I am feeling worn out or discouraged, thinking of Dotty's faith, vigor, and steadfastness often reminds me that the same loving and dependable Guide walks beside me. Her inspiration becomes the syringe of glucose to my jugular. I miss her. Lots of folks miss her!

* * *

Others enter our lives like whirlwinds, making marked impressions and then blow out as abruptly as they came. The young Indian with the striking posture and waist-length gunblue hair is one who left an imprint in my memory. The same guide many of us have come to trust led Gita to her experience on "the hill," but it was a circuitous route. The circumstances surrounding her arrival to His Mansion is quite amazing, but more impressive was Gita's own will to fight an enemy and endure torment in order to win the prize. Gita's name was in my mind and on my tongue long before I actually met her. I first heard of Gita through her dad and the leaders of his church in Yonkers, New York. Years later her name would surface once more.

Dr. and Mrs. Singh wanted the best that America could offer their children--good schools, safe neighborhoods, great friends, and church. But New York City offers both the best and the worst. Gita, despite her Christian parents' desires, chose the latter. Early in my tenure as His Mansion's director, a man from a church in Yonkers called me and asked that we pray for a young woman named Gita. We did. A year later, several churchmen--friends of the Singhs--brought to His Mansion a lovely East Indian woman. She had rebelled against her parents and church, hit the streets, and ended up a drug-addicted prostitute. Her dad had died of heart failure, precipitated, to some extent I am sure, by heartache over his daughter.

Although she was initially excited about the program, Gita soon became angry, nasty, and downright caustic. She rebelled against the rules, resisted prayer, and announced that she hated all of us. In a week's time, however, she seemed transformed. She was growing spiritually and seemed to glow from the change. Several weeks later, she reverted to the dark, hateful person that we recognized from before. The Jekyll and Hyde routine continued. It became evident that the problem was far greater than severe behavioral cycles or physical changes.

Everyone who worked with Gita sensed that she was a special person and that there was an ongoing tug-of-war for her soul. We loved her and were nearly as desperate to see her win this terrifying wrestling match as she was. Having run out of ideas of our own, several of us joined Gita in the prayer room on the second floor of the Mansion. With Bibles in hand and virtually no experience with exorcisms, we began to pray with Gita and read what we believed were appropriate Scriptures. Gita was invited to read with us and to talk about her thoughts and feelings.

The change began as a deep, male, guttural sound percolating up through her throat and out her mouth--growling would be my description of the sound. Words were soon formed out of the growls. They spoke terrible blasphemy and ugly accusations concerning everyone in attendance. Threats of murder and suicide followed. Then the voice cursed and screamed. This went on for an hour or more. Suddenly Gita fell apart. She wept and expressed sorrow for her sinful behavior. She committed herself to walk in the opposite direction. Totally exhausted, Gita returned to her room and slept for more than twelve hours. From then on, life was different for Gita!

Those present have never forgotten the dramatic occurrences, but it is the lessons we learned that have given us strength to press on. Surely some adversary was vying for Gita's will. That was evident. She was a very valuable prize for that entity to torment her mind like that. The devil will go to great lengths to keep a person from following Christ.

It has been a reinforcing source of strength and inspiration to persevere knowing that I, like Gita, am of great value to God.

Gita was a spirited soul. She would sprint across the carpeted lawn with powerful strides, her waist-length, gunblue-black hair streaming behind like a wild horse's mane. That is how I remember her as she broke loose from the bondage of sin and addiction.

After Gita married she volunteered regularly at a center for troubled young people. There was new life and she could expect more of it.

Several years ago Gita, like Miss Dot, took early leave from this world to be with her heavenly Father. One of the needles she'd inserted into her arm while living on the streets of New York, or perhaps as the result of casual sex, introduced the virus that one day awakened to ravage her body. Gita died of AIDS. The enemy may have thought for a fleeting second that he had denied Gita her prize. Foiled again! Gita's soul was possessed of a more powerful Spirit, and she lifted from off the summit to be with God.

* * *

The Apostle Paul exclaimed to a small audience of summit seekers that he was pressing on toward the goal to win the prize for which God had called him heavenward in Christ Jesus. You see, the prize is not earning more than our neighbor, gaining prestige and the respect of our peers--or even "going to heaven." The goal is simply to know God, to walk in fellowship with Him while here on the planet and to finally take one step higher than the highest peek. Therein lies the ultimate prize. Dot Christiansen, Gita Singh, Bill Isaac, and others have already laid hold of the prize while the Shawns, Elmiens, and hundreds of others who have traveled alongside of me on this journey are eagerly climbing upward with hands outstretched.

EPILOGUE
TWO FOOLS ON THE HILL

Sunset from Clark Summit. Knees drawn up against my chest and my chin resting on crossed arms, my mind looks back to the beginning of the adventure. Although I was ignorant of this truth for many years, it has been a spiritual journey all along.

One summer, when I was eight or nine years old a young Jesuit priest accepted an offer to conduct meetings for the youth of St. Christopher's. During his first Saturday session with us, he described Jesus as a compassionate man who loved people—especially children. The passionate priest effectively transported the stone cold Jesus, isolated in a concrete niche in the wall, into a living person who dwelt among us.

God, the Father of Jesus, hated sin according to the priest, and people could not go to heaven where the Father lived because they were contaminated by sin. He went on to say that Jesus loved little children so much that He accepted the punishment for our sin in order that we might be clean enough to be with Him in Heaven. The powerful message of hope lodged itself somewhere in my subconscious, but as I grew older, my conscious mind rehearsed another tune from an old Beatle's album:
> "The man of a thousand voices
> Talking perfectly loud,
> But nobody ever hears him
> Or the sounds he appears to make
> And he never seems to notice..."
A later verse from the same tune goes on to say:
> "but nobody wants to know him."

*   *   *

231

Like most island youngsters, I didn't allot any more time for God than was required, but years later, aboard a submarine 400 feet below the waves of the Atlantic Ocean, all that changed. I heard the message of "The Fool" and wanted nothing more than to know Him.

All of my spare time on the submarine was spent reading the Bible—my guidebook for a new and personal "magical mystery tour." The story of Jesus' journey captivated me. As I walked with Jesus, He became even more personal. His life, as revealed in Scripture, became a rough map for me to follow.

Jesus' teaching and the Bible's practical instruction for life had the ring of truth like nothing else I'd investigated. My imitation of my new role model was poor at best, but the standard never changed. His example has never failed to inspire.

Long before Jesus' final act of sacrifice, He "set his face toward Jerusalem." He could have put a halt to the entire ordeal, but commitment to His Father declared, "not my way, but yours." If temporary separation from His Father were not agony enough, His disciples fell asleep when He needed them most. (So much for community!) His protégé went on to deny that he ever knew Him. Oh, how I can identify with Peter! I trust that the discomfort I feel, as I sit perched on the granite ledge, is the pain of a tender conscience.

The road inclined steeply before Jesus at this juncture. He knew as others could not, that the going was about to get ugly. Yet he persevered. Onlookers spit and jeered. Jesus loved them.

> "But nobody wants to know him,
> They can see he's just a fool.
> And he never gives an answer,"

*   *   *

*　*　*

Even as I gaze into the brilliance of a sunset I see the valley before as through clouded lenses. There is so much to be appreciated. Those who sat gazing at Jesus from afar and saw only the cross resigned themselves to defeat. But Jesus had the ultimate view. From His vantage point, suspended between heaven and earth, He could see the empty tomb, which three days hence would declare "Victory!" to the whole world. He is the Sunshine!

Life has been an adventure. The preparation, the launching out, and the steady climb have been arduous but rewarding. The view from the top is exhilarating. Our Guide knew all along that the trip would be hard enough if we carried no load, but with the awful weight of our sin it would be unbearable. Jesus offered to bear that burden when He made the invitation: "Come to me all you who labor and are heavy laden, and I will give you rest." He promised not only rest, but also resurrection: "Now if we died with Christ, we believe that we will also live with Him!"

Life may appear like a random set of billiard-ball collisions—I know it did to me at one time—but the truth be known, we really never choose Him, He chooses us. The very same way Jesus chose the disciples—not because of whom they were but because of who he knew they would become—He chooses us.

There is but a glow remaining as the spot where I sit today gradually bids adieu to ol' Sol. For those just starting out on their life journey it is not seen as setting but as a bright, new beginning. The mountain beckons. The road before you leads to deep ravines, treacherous canyons, and tumultuous currents. It is a part of the experience. But the road also brings you through villages filled with life, magnificent vistas, and intense joy. I've savored these as well.

233

In our beginnings and our endings, God is with us. He will not forsake us. God has chosen the "foolish" of this world to confound the wise. From the start, I, we, are but broken pots of clay, but in these vessels we carry about with us the glory of God. Out through the cracks spills the light of the world.

*　*　*

"But the fool on the hill
Sees the sun going down"

As darkness lays claim and the night air becomes deathly quiet, a fool listens for that still, small voice saying: "Well done...welcome home!"

THE END

Additional copies of FOOL ON A HILL may be obtained by selecting the following options:

1. Purchase on the web at: <www.bellbuoy.com> (preferred)

2. Sending order with check or money order to: Bellbuoy Books, PO BOX 624, Hillsboro, NH 03244.

3. Request that your local bookstore carry it. They may order from Bellbuoy Books (division of Tidal-Tail Books LLC), PO BOX 624, Hillsboro, NH 03244

4. E-mail your order to <stan@bellbuoy.com > and your order will be shipped with an invoice. You may pay by check or money order.

> FOOL ON A HILL lists for $12.00 per copy
> Six to twelve copies, $9.00
> Twelve plus, $8.00
> Postage & Handling: $1.50/ea up to five; $1.00/ea.
> Check web page for special rates.

Bulk rates for retail and/or conferences, contact publisher by e-mail. Author available for speaking engagements and autograph sessions. Individual autographed copies upon request.